Godthinks**you're**an

Whodo**you**think**you**are**?**

SteveMawston

Scripture Union, 207–209 Queensway, Bletchley, MK2 2EB, England.

First published 1997

ISBN 1 85999 203 X

British Library Cataloguing-in-Publication Data
A catalogue record for this book is available from the British Library.

Scripture quotations are from (1) the Contemporary English Version Bible, copyright © 1997 British and Foreign Bible Society, Old and New Testament © 1991, 1992, 1995; (2) The Holy Bible New International Version, copyright © 1973, 1978, 1984 by International Bible Society, anglicisation copyright © 1979, 1984, 1989, used by permission of Hodder and Stoughton Limited.

Cover design by ie DESIGN.

Printed and bound in Great Britain by Cox & Wyman Ltd, Reading.

CONTENTS

NB *The names of the young people who contributed to this book have been changed.*

AUTHOR PROFILE

Name? Steve Mawston

No middle names? OK , it's William!

Job? I work with young people in an inner-city school. Definitely not a teacher. More a cross between a youth minister and a school counsellor. Basically, I help young people sort out their problems – and get paid!

How long for? 5 years.

Hobbies? Sport – basketball, football, cricket and (sadly) golf. I love travelling too.

Passions? Middlesbrough FC. My gorgeous wife, Rachel. Speaking to young people about this sort of stuff.

Embarrassing moments? Not being able to get the film out of my camera at the end of my honeymoon. I asked the girl in the photo-shop to help, only to be told, 'But, sir, there isn't any film in here…'

1 WHO DO YOU THINK YOU ARE?

I'll never forget the first time I played football for Ferryhill Wednesday.

It was the local under-19s team, and I was just thirteen when the manager selected me. On the day of the first game I arrived early, and was ushered into the changing rooms. My new team mates were all several years older than me and a pretty mean-looking bunch. I was tall for my age but I had the physique of a stick insect.

Alan, the captain, was regarded as a bit of a hero. He looked me up and down suspiciously. 'Well, I hope you can play a bit,' he said.

Something told me he wasn't too convinced.

I stood nervously with the manager as the game began. (I was the substitute.) It was a windy day and the pitch was in an exposed position on top of a hill. To add to our difficulties, the team we were playing were one of the best in the league. By half-time we were already 3-0 down.

Ten minutes into the second half my services were required. The ball had gone out for a corner, so the manager signalled to the referee and pulled off one of our central defenders. I sprinted onto the pitch, back to my own box, and was told by Alan to mark a player near the front post.

This was my chance to show what I was made of. Whatever happened, I was determined the opposition weren't going to score from *this* corner kick. As the opposing winger prepared to take the corner, my legs felt like jelly. I really needed to impress my new team, particularly Alan.

When the kick was taken, the ball came towards me. In that split second I pictured myself rising above my opponent and heading it back to safety for another corner. But, as I jumped into the air, the ball oscillated slightly in the wind and grazed off the side of my head. Instead of heading it away, this slight but devastatingly effective contact resulted in the ball flying into the top corner – for one truly spectacular own goal.

My team-mates stared at me open-mouthed, not knowing whether I'd realised which way we were kicking. One or two of them laughed. I wanted the ground to swallow me up.

For the rest of the match I performed moderately well, but I'd already blown it. Back in the dressing room I heard a few of the players having a laugh about my debut performance. I quickly got my stuff together, said 'Bye' to the manager and headed home feeling about two inches tall. All the time a voice inside my head kept saying, 'What a failure. You made a complete idiot of yourself this time. You're just an embarrassment.'

Why do I feel so bad?

I'm sure you have been in a similar position at some time yourself. The people may have been different, the incident may have been different, but the voice in your head and the feelings were much the same. One girl wrote to me recently:

When I was bullied I felt as though I was living in a nightmare, only this one you couldn't wake up out of and think, 'Oh it was only a dream.' The bully made me believe I was a useless, degraded being. I felt rejected by my peers, some of whom were supposed to be my friends. It was as though a conspiracy was taking place. Whenever people laughed or joked, I thought they were having a go at me. I got very paranoid and felt depressed and isolated.

Psychologists say such feelings arise out of low self-esteem, or a lack of self-worth. But what exactly does this mean?

Imagine I asked you the following three questions. How would you answer them on a scale of 0 ('I'm a complete waste of space') to 10 ('Yes, I am incredibly valuable')?

Do you think you are worth anything?...........................
Do you have any value? ....
Do you think you are important? ....
Total ....

If you scored between 0 and 15, you have very low self-esteem and don't value yourself as much as you should.

If you scored between 15 and 25, you think you're an OK sort of person, but you probably go through times when you don't feel you're worth very much.

If you scored over 25, you have high self-esteem. Great! Very few young people have such a positive view of themselves. However, there are dangers, as we shall see.

Obviously these scores aren't set in granite for all time. They will vary according to your mood and the kind of day you're having. It's quite normal to feel good about yourself one moment and then suddenly to feel depressed. After all, your emotions are about as easy to manage as a bank account when you're living on a student grant! But some people don't just feel bad, they believe they *are* bad. These people (and maybe you're one of them) find it very difficult to see themselves as valuable and of worth at any time. There are others, of course, who seem to have a bit of an ego problem. They go around acting like a Rottweiler with attitude, as if the world revolves around them. To see the difference between a person with a seriously inflated ego and one with healthy self-esteem, picture the following scene.

You're at a crowded party. The music is kicking, your mates are on the dance floor, you're sat munching on a plate of Worcester sauce crisps and pickled onions. In walks a seriously attractive member of the opposite sex. Do you:

a Sit there, trying desperately to think of a way of introducing yourself, but convinced that she/he can probably smell your breath from the other side of the room?

B Pop a polo in your mouth, cruise over confidently and whisper into her/his ear, 'You should be kissed. Often. And by someone who knows how.' Then smile expectantly?

C Decide she/he is someone worth getting to know, and make a point of going over and introducing yourself when the time is right?

If you resemble person A, you probably suffer from low

self-esteem. If you are person B, it sounds like you suffer from an ego problem. But God doesn't want us to be either of those two extremes. The Bible says, 'Do not think of yourself more highly than you ought...' (Romans 12:3).

The key to having a healthy self-esteem is to see yourself as God sees you, no more and no less. A biblical view of yourself isn't built on your experience of life but on your experience of God. Ultimately, the important question isn't so much who *you* think you are but what *God* thinks of you. This is what this book is really all about – helping you see things from his perspective. By the time you have finished reading it, you'll have discovered:

- How to build your view of yourself on what God thinks of you rather than on the way you feel or the way others treat you.

And along the way:

- What influences the way you feel about yourself.
- How to deal with feelings of low self-worth.
- How to increase your confidence without developing an ego problem.

2 WHO'S PULLING YOUR STRINGS?

A famous pop star was taking part in a fund-raising event for charity. He was used to having crowds scream and drool whenever he made a public appearance (and that was just the men!).

The story goes that at this particular function he began to get rather irritated when he found himself near the end of a very long queue for lunch. As each person held out their plate, they were served by a group of elderly helpers.

The pop star collected salad, quiche, a bread roll and a piece of butter from the old dear on the end. As it happened, he had a particular liking for butter and he not very politely demanded a second piece.

The elderly waitress was blissfully unaware of his identity. Glancing down the line and seeing there were still a lot of people waiting to be served, she replied, 'I'm sorry, sir, only one piece of butter per person.'

The pop star scowled. 'Do you know who I am?' he asked.

Leaning forward slightly, the old lady whispered, 'Do you know who *I* am?'

'No,' he replied.

'I'm the one with the butter, sonny, so move on!'

Will the real me please step forward?

Have you ever stopped to ask yourself, 'Who am I? Who is the *real* me? What influences the way I see myself?'

Admittedly, these aren't the sort of things you ponder when you're lined up in the dinner queue. Or at least you may *think* they're not. In fact, we ask ourselves questions like these continually without really being aware of doing so ('subconsciously' is the technical term for all you psychology buffs). The answers we get are incredibly important. Before you go any further in this chapter, take a couple of minutes to do the following exercise. It will help you learn about the way you see yourself. Write down the first answers that come into your mind. You can think more about them afterwards. For example, here are some answers I might give:

I am tall.
I am good at football (usually).
I am a hopeless dancer.
I am a naff singer.

Who am I?

I am...
I am...
I am...
I am...
I am...
I am...
I am...
I am...
I am...
I am...

Looking back through your list, see which answers are positive and which are generally negative. For example, if you have put 'I am fat', that's pretty negative so place a minus sign − next to your answer. If you have written, 'I am happy', that's a fairly positive answer so give it a +. Some of your answers will be neutral because they are merely descriptive ('I am 16 years old' is really neither negative nor positive).

This exercise should help you learn more about whether you have high or low self-esteem.

What's it all about?
• • • • • • • • • • • • • • • • •

What are the factors that influence the way we see ourselves? How come self-confidence oozes out of some people, while others walk around with a chip on their shoulder believing the whole world's against them?

Basically, there are loads of factors that affect the way we see ourselves. The following are just a few of them.

PARENTS

Ellen was pretty, intelligent and had loads of friends. During a routine visit to the school nurse she broke down in tears and told the nurse how depressed she had been recently. The subject came round to her parents.

Ellen's father was a very successful businessman. She only saw him every two weeks, as her parents had divorced and she was living with her mum. Whenever they met, he asked Ellen how she was getting on at school. She told him things were going well and that she had got good results in her Key Stage 3 tests. In fact in maths she had scored over 80%. Ellen expected her father to be proud of her, but he only asked, 'Was that the highest in the class?'

She replied that it was the second highest.

'Next time make sure you're first.'

Her dad didn't encourage Ellen at all. As far as he was concerned, she felt, she simply hadn't done well enough. It was through talking to the school nurse that she began to see that her identity was being shaped by the way her dad treated her. He would only be pleased if she got the top mark. Only by pleasing him would she feel good about herself.

Our parents' expectations can be like a high jump bar. Whenever we do well, more is expected of us and the bar is raised a little higher. Eventually it gets so high that we become scared and daren't even attempt it in case we fail or get hurt. We tell ourselves, 'I just can't do it. I'm not good enough. It's beyond me.'

We are all affected by the kind of relationship we have with our parents. Not just by their expectations of us either. The things they say to us, the amount of time we spend with them, the way they treat us, the amount of love and praise they give us, all have a massive impact on the way we see ourselves.

The problem is that parents aren't perfect. They are frail and vulnerable human beings who make mistakes. As a result, many young people carry with them feelings of pain, resentment, hurt and anger at the way they have been treated. Statistics show, horrifyingly, that 1 in 10 young people have been abused in some way by their parents.

If your parents have divorced or if one (or both) has died, this will also have a significant impact on the way you feel about yourself. Reading this section may stir up strong, painful emotions. If so, make sure you talk to someone you trust, like a minister, a youth worker, someone who has experience in counselling or in helping people with their problems, or perhaps Childline. They will be able to help you deal with the particular issue that is affecting you and the way you feel about yourself as a result. But you may need to give it some time.

Question

Can you think of a time when your parents directly influenced the way you felt about yourself? Has your parents' influence generally been positive or negative?

BODIES

Everyone has something about the way they look that they don't like. For me as a teenager, it was my nose – a generously proportioned feature clearly inherited from my father's genetic pool. Fortunately, since then my body has grown considerably (I am now six foot five) while my nose has stayed much the same.

It's easy to get obsessed with one aspect of your physical appearance, whether it's your nose, your chest, your teeth, your eyes or another part of your anatomy. You convince yourself you make Quasimodo look like Tom Cruise. One 'bad' feature dominates the way you see yourself, and you label yourself 'ugly' and 'unattractive.' It could be that your hair is totally unmanageable or your ears have a passing resemblance to the FA Cup. Whatever the problem, you feel angry at God for failing to pay attention when you were being put together. You imagine other people are watching your every move to see whether or not you're an acceptable member of the human race.

A survey by *Psychology Today* found that 62% of teenage girls didn't like their bodies. The number one reason for this was because they were overweight. When questioned how many years of life they would trade in order to be slimmer, 15% answered five or more! The conclusion we could draw from this is that some people believe life is only worth living if you're thin (David Garner, PhD, 'Body Image Survey Results', February 1997, p36).

Question

How do you see your body? Do you feel generally positive or negative about it? How big an impact does your body image have on the way you see yourself?

Of course, it's not just our body image that affects us. The way we treat our bodies plays a big part in how we feel about them. As the proverb says, 'A healthy body promotes a healthy mind'. Treat your body badly and you will feel the pits. Treat it well and you will feel a lot more cheerful and confident! Just as a car needs things like petrol, oil and water to run well, so your body requires proper sleep, diet and exercise.

Are you getting enough sleep? My wife will tell you that I get really stroppy when I'm tired. Making sure you get seven or eight hours a night fairly frequently can mean you have a much more positive outlook on life. Do you exercise regularly? (Five minutes staggering to and from the bus-stop each day is probably not going to hone your body to school sports, never mind Olympic, performance standards.) And does your diet contain plenty of fresh fruit and non-chip-like vegetables?

Preparing for the times when you are likely to be under stress is a good idea. Many women are affected by PMT. If you know it's the massive hormonal changes that go on inside your body at this time of the month that are responsible for (a) your mood swings, (b) your lower flip-out threshold and (c) your heightened awareness of your body's imperfections, you'll be better able to cope!

Question
What are the physical factors that affect the way you see yourself?

THE MEDIA MAKES ME MAD

We are constantly bombarded with messages from the media. Advertising alone is a multi-million pound business, and its sole aim is to entice the general public into buying particular products by whatever means necessary.

Let's face it. It works. When Levi's produced the advert with the 'hunk' stripping down to his boxers and putting his jeans into the washing machine, sales of Levis went up 700%.

Advertisers achieve their objective by splattering our screens with images of the ideal body. It doesn't matter what the product is – everything from chocolate bars to cars to washing machines includes perfect curves, complexions and cheek-bones. The underlying message is 'If you buy this perfume, you too will have the allure of Kate Moss' or 'If you drive this car, women will fall at your feet.'

Unfortunately, advertising has a dangerous side-effect. Normal people like us compare our bodies to those of the models we see in adverts, on movie screens or in magazines, and we think, 'Hey, I don't look like that!' The media screams at our subconscious, 'You're not good enough, you're ugly. You need to look like this, mate!'

Recently there has been something of a moral back-lash against this. It's no longer possible to deny that the supermodel/ideal body culture has a negative effect on the way people feel about themselves. Three out of ten people questioned by *Psychology Today* said they felt angry, four out of ten that they felt insecure as a result of media brainwashing on the way we should look.

Try an experiment next time you're watching TV. When the adverts come on, see how many use physical beauty to attract you to buying the product. Look out for a stunning model, some hero looking like Brad Pitt or a scantily clad female. The message is 'Buying this product will make you like this person. Buying this product will help you attract members of the opposite sex. Buying this product will make you desirable to these kinds of people.'

These adverts are saying to us that only physical qualities matter. There is no mention of personality, sense of humour, intelligence, love, compassion, sensitivity – all important parts of being human. Adverts grossly exaggerate the importance of physical attractiveness. (It's worth bearing in mind that models often spend at least three hours getting made-up, and when they appear on magazine covers most of their zits will have been erased by computer! You could probably do a pretty good job on anyone given three hours and a powerful PC!)

So the media presents an ideal, a standard against which we measure ourselves. Girls, if thin is in and you happen to have a curvy figure, then tough. Lads, if the mags say designer stubble is hot and you're still on your first disposable razor, there's not much you can do.

Question
How big an influence does the media have on the way you see yourself?

PERFORMANCE
'I'm useless.'
    'I'm average.'
    'Well, I suppose I'm quite good really.'

Some people see their identity in terms of their performance. Often the most popular and confident people at school are those who are good academically or at sport. For those who are more practically minded or who can't seem to co-ordinate their bodily movements, lessons/PE can be a nightmare.

I remember playing in a basketball match at school against Sedgefield Comprehensive. They had a superb football team and always beat us soundly. However, we were the league champions at basketball, and for months I looked forward to us getting our revenge. When it came to the actual match, it was a disaster. Nothing seemed to go right and we lost by one point. Afterwards, in the changing rooms, I felt totally gutted. Looking back, I can see that I was basing my identity on my performance.

People who are performance-oriented constantly compare themselves to others. They don't like being beaten in exams, at sport or even in 'friendly' games. In church everything they do has to be good, whether they're part of the singing group or the coffee-after-the-service team.

Sometimes people want to do well because they are naturally competitive. However, they may be motivated by many other things, including the need for reassurance or approval from others, such as parents, peers, even God. Unfortunately we all make mistakes and fail. For performance-oriented people life is a cruise – as long as they're winning. Defeat or a poor performance knocks their self-esteem for six. It can leave them feeling completely worthless. They make the mistake of measuring who they are in terms of how they do.

Question

How much of an influence does your performance have on the way you see yourself? In what areas are

you competitive? Sport? Academic achievements?
Others?

THE PAST

Emma was one of those girls everyone liked. She was friendly, warm and attractive. She often brought friends along to church. She sang in the music group. She was always there if a job needed doing. Emma was like a spiritual reservoir, constantly pouring out to others.

Emma started going out with one of the lads in the youth group. Mark hadn't been coming for long, but he seemed to be a committed Christian. Things went fine at first, then Mark started to touch Emma in places she had never been touched before. It felt incredible. Afterwards, she would be overcome with guilt and want to tell him they must stop. But somehow she never plucked up the courage. Soon Emma became pregnant.

When her parents found out, they went ballistic. Pretty soon the minister knew, and the youth leader and half the church. Two months later Emma had a miscarriage.

Emma still goes to church, but she and Mark split up shortly after she lost the baby. Nobody remembers what happened three years ago. Her parents never mention it and everyone at church thinks the world of her. But inside Emma still suffers. A voice says, 'You're dirty. It's your fault that Michelle (the name Emma gave to the baby) died. God will never love you again after what you've done.' No matter how well things go for Emma, her past continues to haunt her. It's as if her whole life has been tainted by that one episode.

Each of us is influenced by our past – the way we were brought up, the things we have done, the things others have done to us.

How big an influence does the past have on the way you see yourself? Are there incidents you can identify as having particular importance?

THE POWER OF PEER PRESSURE

A while ago I visited a school in Cleveland, in the north-east of England, to take some RE lessons. One of the topics I was given was 'peer pressure'. I decided to use an idea from James Dobson, a respected teacher and writer in the United States, to illustrate what 'peer pressure' means.

I announced the subject to the class. At this point Paul, one of the students, asked if he could leave the lesson for five minutes as he had an appointment with another member of staff. I gave him permission – his absence provided me with an excellent opportunity.

While he was gone, I briefed the rest of the class on the plan. When Paul returned I would continue with the lesson as normal and then after a few minutes announce that we would have a mental arithmetic test. The question would be 'What is 8 times 7? Is it (a) 50 (b) 56 or (c) 64?' Rather than answer correctly with (b), I wanted the class to put their hands up on (c).

When Paul returned, we swung into action.

'Right, time for a spot of mental arithmetic. What is 8 times 7? Is it (a) 50 (b) 56 or (c) 64? OK, everyone who thinks 8 times 7 is 50, hands up.'

There was silence. Paul sat there looking slightly bemused, thinking to himself, 'Doesn't this guy realise he's speaking to a top set? Everyone knows 8 times 7 is 56!'

Nobody put their hand up.

'OK, everyone who thinks 8 times 7 is 56.'

Immediately Paul's hand shot into the air. Then he looked around the room. No one else had their hand up! Some of the class stared at him, others tried hard not to snigger.

Paul furiously went through his seven times table. One seven is seven, two sevens are fourteen, three sevens are twenty-one ... (his hand is slowly going down) ... seven sevens are forty-nine, eight sevens are ... (he looks around one more time) ... eight sevens are fifty ... They can't be ... (his hand drops to his side).

Paul's classmates are dying to explode, but it isn't over yet.

'OK, everyone who thinks that 8 times 7 is 64.'

Immediately every hand goes up in perfect unison. Paul is desperately trying to get his brain back in gear.

'Eight times seven is *not* sixty-four ... (he looks around) ... It can't be ... (he feels his hand begin to gravitate vertically) ... It must be. His hand goes right up into the air.

All of us have been Paul at some stage in our lives, whether we're aware of it or not. Peer pressure affects every one of us, not just young people. It has a bearing on the way we dress, the way we speak and the way we act. There are certain unwritten rules that if you want to be 'in' you have to, for example, wear a particular brand of trainers. Anyone who wears trainers that aren't the right make is considered a complete geek. It's not that the 'right' trainers enhance sporting performance or give you the edge on the basketball or tennis court. That has absolutely nothing to do with it. It's peer pressure.

THE EFFECTS OF PEER PRESSURE

Peer pressure encourages us to compare ourselves to those around us. Our value, our worth, is determined by how good we look beside them. When you get your exam results, it's not just how well you do that counts: it's how well you do compared to the rest of your class.

We compare ourselves in lots of ways.

'Why is it that Jade always has a perfect complexion when National Geographic could do a feature on my zits?'

'How come Rodney can do everything? He never seems to put a foot wrong in sport, he sails through his exams though he never revises, and there isn't a girl who doesn't fancy him.'

Peer pressure also affects the way we behave. We want to impress those around us, to have their admiration (though we may find it hard to admit this to ourselves). Unfortunately, we all sometimes do stupid things – things that just *do not* go down well in a group situation. I remember the time I went on a school trip and sat on a banana all the way there without realising it. The effects of this were apparent to my fellow pupils within seconds of me stepping off the coach.

More recently, a student at the school I work in came in wearing uniform on a non-uniform day. He got teased so badly, he stormed out of a lesson and ended up in tears in my room. He had failed to observe the unwritten rules that peer pressure lays down.

Question

Can you think of a time when you did something that wasn't the thing to do in a group situation?

Often we respond by feeling inadequate, ashamed and totally stupid. We hear a voice inside our heads, whispering, 'You're hopeless. What a loser. Everyone thinks you're a complete joke. Why do you always have to embarrass yourself?'

At first these statements are flimsy labels we stick on ourselves. They are temporary; the glue soon dries up and they fall off. However, over a period of time the labels may start to stick rather more effectively. They can begin to become a part of our identity: 'I'll never be any good. I'm a failure. What a loser I am.'

One reason peer pressure is so powerful is that we tend to *believe* what others say about us. Let me illustrate what I mean.

When I was fifteen I joined a choir. Up till that point I had always told people I couldn't sing. Of course, I didn't necessarily expect them to believe me! The truth is, I wasn't actually that bad. On a scale of 0 to 10, I suppose I was a 5 or 6. Anyway, our choir was recruiting new members so I agreed to go along. As my reputation went before me, everyone had a bit of a laugh when I turned up at the first choir practice.

'What are you doing here, oh tuneless one?'

Others made jokes about not wanting to stand near me.

I didn't think too much about it – until one or two people made comments they seemed to mean. I began to wonder if I could sing after all, or if perhaps they were right – I wasn't actually a 5, but a 2 or a 1.

I listened to what people said, I believed it, I allowed it to become part of my identity. 'I can sing a bit' became 'I can't sing'. The result was that I dropped out of the choir. You see, our behaviour tends to fall in line with the way we see ourselves, our sense of personal identity.

My mistake was in *believing* what others said about me. This is why it's so important to be sure of who we are. We need to have a strong foundation on which to build our identity.

Question
How big an influence does peer pressure have on the way you see yourself? Can you identify an occasion when peer pressure affected you?

Exercise

Look back at the answers you have given to the questions in each section. Which factor would you say has the strongest influence on the way you see yourself? Give each a rating of 1 to 6 (1 being the biggest influence and 6 being the weakest).

Parents   [   ]
Bodies   [   ]
Media   [   ]
Performance   [   ]
Past   [   ]
Peers   [   ]

I hope this chapter has helped you see that there are lots of things which may influence the way we feel about ourselves. I have only covered some of the main ones. Looking through the list above, how do you feel now about building your view of yourself on such things?

Now, let's imagine person X.

X wasn't treated well by his parents, doesn't perform well at school and isn't much of a looker. How does X feel about himself? Will he have to go through life feeling like this? Could there be a firmer foundation on which he might build his view of himself? That's the subject of the next chapter.

3 FOUNDATIONS

Two men owned construction businesses. Both decided to build new houses for their families. The first man was a bit of a cheapskate and, cutting as many corners as he did, it was no surprise that his house was up in a flash. Everyone in the village came to celebrate and, in the evenings that followed, the man would sit on the veranda in his rocking chair, contentedly enjoying the cool air as he watched his neighbour sweat and toil next door.

It took the second builder months of hard work, preparing the ground and putting in foundations, before he could even start on the house. (He was one of those 'if a thing's worth doing, it's worth doing well' kind of blokes.) But eventually his house was finished and he too threw a party.

Both houses looked great.

A few weeks later there was a major storm which caused devastation throughout the neighbourhood. The second builder awoke the next morning to the sound of his neighbour pounding on the door.

During the night the storm had blown his whole house away, and destroyed all his possessions. He had nothing left.

This story (which you will no doubt recognise as the parable of the wise man who built his house on the rock and the foolish man who made do with something rather less substantial) was told by Jesus to get over to us an important principle: what we build on matters. Rock (a strong foundation) is good; sand (an inadequate foundation that's liable to collapse when the going gets a bit stormy) ain't.

What foundation are you building on?

In the last chapter we looked at the different factors that influence the way we feel about ourselves. There's no doubt our sense of worth can be bolstered by the fact that our parents care deeply about us or that we have loads of friends. Love is, after all, incredibly important, and we all need to be loved. But human love is, unfortunately, imperfect.

OK, so you're popular with your mates now, but what happens if you fall out with them? And building your sense of self-esteem on what your parents think of you can be a disaster. If they love and appreciate you, that's great. But I've met many people who have spent their whole lives trying to earn their parents' approval and to live up to their expectations. No matter how hard they try, they never get the affirmation they're desperate for.

The truth is, people are just not a strong enough foundation on which to build your sense of self-worth.

Research bears this out. Psychologists agree that for healthy human development people need to be praised more than they are put down. Statistics show that by the time you are 18, you will have received on average 25,000 words of encouragement. If you're wondering why most teenagers aren't walking around with swollen egos, it's because you get most of these before you are 3! And listen to this – by the age of 18, the average person will also have received around 225,000 put-downs, almost 10 times as many. If you're relying on the approval of others to build your self-esteem on, don't bother!

The other factors we looked at in the last chapter are equally unreliable. For example, take body image. You may look stunning now, but a sudden spurt of acne can swiftly transform the most perfect of complexions into something resembling a pizza. And, while a few people do get more attractive as they get older, sadly most of us battle with wrinkly bits and droopy bits and hair going grey or simply disappearing altogether.

Take a look at the lives of supermodels. You would think that if anybody had high self-esteem, they would. Surely with all that beauty and wealth, the world is at your feet? Yet what do we find? Naomi Campbell allegedly trying to commit suicide after a row with her Flamenco-dancing boyfriend, who is reported as saying elsewhere that she comes a long way behind his career and is not actually the kind of girl he intends to marry anyway. The truth is, there's a lot more to life and relationships than physical attractiveness. Building your self-worth on the way you look is like building on sand. It's foolish.

A new foundation

Right, so you may be convinced that you need to build on a sound foundation. But how does 'rock' translate into everyday life? Some practical guidelines might be helpful.

In chapter one I said that a healthy view of yourself

is built on what God thinks of you, not on your own experience of life. The aim is to see yourself 'as God sees you'. How on earth do we do that?

Well, in the next few chapters, we will be looking at what God says in the Bible about our worth and value. You might like to think of these things as individual rocks you can build on. The more rocks you can find to support you, the more secure you will feel in God's love (and, incidentally, the less it will matter what the world thinks about you!).

Still seems a bit vague? Perhaps it would help to look at the life of Jesus. How did he cope with living in the world?

He was born with the stigma of being illegitimate in the eyes of his community. He obviously had an attractive personality: 'People liked him, and he pleased God' (Luke 2:52). But perhaps this only made his rejection by the people he had grown up with all the more shocking. When he returned to Nazareth to preach, 'they got up, forced Jesus out of town, and took him to the edge of the cliff on which the town was built. They meant to throw him off the edge' (Luke 4:29).

He was betrayed by Judas, denied by Peter, attacked relentlessly by Satan and persecuted by the religious leaders who sought to murder him. Perhaps most painful of all, he was mocked by the very crowds who, when he entered Jerusalem, had greeted him with joy, waving palm branches and shouting with praise. If Jesus had built his view of himself on his experience of life and on how others treated him, I think there would have been plenty of scope for clinical depression!

In fact, if you look at the things Jesus said about himself, you will see that he seems to display both remarkable confidence and humility at the same time. Take the following, for example:

> 'I am the light for the world! Follow me, and you
> won't be walking in the dark. You will have the light
> that gives life.' *(John 8:12)*
> 'I am the way and the truth and the life. No-one
> comes to the Father except through me.' *(John 14:6)*

How could Jesus say these things? Because his sense of
worth didn't come from his experience of life but from
his relationship with his Father in heaven.

> 'The one who sent me is with me; he has not left
> me alone, for I always do what pleases him.'
> *(John 8:29)*

Jesus believed that God was with him even when people
were treating him badly, and this helped him to cope.
Furthermore, he didn't actually worry about impress-
ing those around him. He was more concerned about
pleasing God. So it didn't matter that they didn't think
he was the greatest thing since (to go back to the
future) sliced bread.

Particularly affirming to Jesus was an incident that
took place just as he was beginning his teaching min-
istry. He came down from Galilee to the Jordan to be
baptised by his cousin, John. John tried to put him off:
'You should be the one baptising me, not the other way
round. *You're* the big shot around here – you've been
sent by God to save the world'. But Jesus persisted, and
eventually John baptised him. As soon as he came up
out of the water an incredible thing happened:

> ...the Holy Spirit came down upon him in the
> form of a dove. A voice from heaven said, 'You
> are my own dear Son, and I am pleased with you.'
> *(Luke 3:22)*

This was the Father saying who Jesus was: 'my own dear Son'. Jesus was quite clear about his identity but, more than that, he knew his Father loved him. He was able to keep going through rejection, pain and suffering because his identity was built on the relationship he had with his Father God. He is the perfect example of what it means to build your house on rock.

Straight talk
••••••••••••

As I write this book, I am very conscious that some of you have not had an easy life. Sometimes as I listen to young people talk about the things they have been through, I feel desperately sorry for them. I have never experienced some of the situations that increasing numbers of young people have to deal with – abuse, parents divorcing, the death of someone very close, being raped, feeling suicidal, being caught up in self-harm. Neither can I promise you that you'll have a happy, problem-free future. It's not quite so simple as 'Live for God, and life will be a bed of roses'.

What I can say is that whether you have had a relatively easy existence or whether your life has been tough, nothing beats basing your view of yourself on your relationship with God and on what he says about you.

It's time to look for some rocks…

4 WONDERFULLY AND MARVELLOUSLY MADE

Creation
• • • • • • • •

The best-selling book in the history of the world begins
with a dramatic story. It is the story of the unveiling of
a masterpiece, the genesis or the beginning of life, the
history of creation.

> In the beginning God
> created the heavens
>   and the earth.
> The earth was barren,
>   with no form of life;
> it was under a roaring ocean
>   covered with darkness.
> But the Spirit of God
>   was moving over the water.
>
> God said, 'I command light to shine!' And light
> started shining. God looked at the light and saw that
> it was good. He separated light from darkness and
> named the light 'Day' and the darkness 'Night'.
> (Genesis 1:1–5)

On the second day God made the sky, and on the third
day he created the dry land and the sea. The land produced vegetation, plants and trees. After three days
of divine endeavour, God sat back and surveyed his

creation, and he saw that 'it was good'.

On the fourth day God placed the sun and the moon in their orbits, the stars and planets throughout the vast universe.

On the fifth day, he fashioned all the creatures of the sea and the birds of the air.

On the sixth, after the earth is filled with all sorts of animals, the story reaches its crescendo:

So God created humans to be like himself; he made men and women. *(Genesis 1:27)*

Then God surveyed the work of his hands, all that he had made. And this time he pronounced it as '*very* good' (v31).

Before, when God had looked at the slowly rising sun, at the full moon, at the stars illuminating the first night sky, he had said that they were 'good'. The spectacular Himalayan mountain range, the rain forests, the brilliantly coloured birds, the beautiful (and, frankly, sometimes rather peculiar) animals, were all pronounced 'good'. But after God had made man and woman (you and me), the world became 'very good'.

If there had been an interviewer there on the seventh day, and he had asked God, 'Tell me, of all the things you've just made, which is the one you're most proud of? Which do you value the most?', what do you think God would have said?

'You!!'

So, what does God think of us humans? What does he think of *me?* In the drama of creation we were the highlight, the pinnacle, the crescendo, the best bit – like the final burst of fireworks on Bonfire Night. We weren't something he was embarrassed about. He didn't want to hide us away to stop anyone else from seeing us (like when you're going out with someone and you're worried your mates may think she/he is a bit of a dork). No, we were the final touch to the masterpiece. We made the difference between 'good' and 'very good'.

Made in his image
• • • • • • • • • • • • • • • •
Why are we so special? The answer lies in Genesis 1:26 – because we are made in the image of God. This means that human beings are not just advanced apes, one step further along the evolutionary scale than the rest of the animal kingdom. The fact is, only human beings have minds with the capacity to make moral choices. Only human beings have spirits, and the capacity to know God and build a relationship with him. This is the first rock on which we can build our view of ourselves:

Genesis 1:26

I am made in the image of God.

His workmanship
• • • • • • • • • • • • • • • •
Well, it's been a nice idyll in the garden of Eden (we haven't yet got to the bit where things start to go wrong), but how does this relate to us today? Moving on (a bit) to the first century, here's the apostle Paul writing to the Christians in Ephesus:

> For we are God's workmanship, created in Christ Jesus to do good works, which God prepared in advance for us to do. (Ephesians 2:10)

We will look at the second half of this statement a little later. For now, let's turn the first half into an 'I am' statement:

> 'I am God's workmanship. I have been individually created by him.'

Now 'workmanship' may not be one of the top five thousand words in your vocabulary, so what's Paul trying to get across to us here?

He is painting a picture of a God who is an artist. 'Workmanship' is derived from the Greek word poeima, from which we get our word 'poem'. Think about it – you are a poem written by God (well, you literary types might find this appealing!). The important thing is that you are a work of art, a unique individual made by God.

Have you ever considered that there never has been and never will be another person just like you? For example, new technology is being developed which may replace PIN numbers and cards in the next ten years. When you want to take money out of your account, you simply place your hand in the hole in the wall. A computer will trace the two hundred scents which your body releases, and check the combination of these to see if the cash can be safely dispensed. Each of us is unique in terms of the way we smell – and in many other ways, including the design of our fingerprints. (In eighty years of fingerprint testing the Metropolitan Police have never found two prints the same.) You could say, going back to our 'work of art' illustration, that 'when God finished making me, he threw away the mould'.

You are valuable

Several times in the Gospels Jesus spoke of the worth of individual human beings. Here are some examples:

'Aren't two sparrows sold for only a penny? But your Father knows when any one of them falls to the ground. Even the hairs on your head are counted. So don't be afraid! You are worth much more than many sparrows.' *(Matthew 10:29–31)*

'Look at the birds in the sky! They don't plant or harvest. They don't even store grain in barns. Yet your Father in heaven takes care of them. Aren't you worth more than birds?' *(Matthew 6:26)*

Get this! Jesus is saying that God is a Father who values you as an individual. He knows you intimately. He is aware of details like the number of hairs on your head. He knows all the things you have done, both good and bad, including those things that no one else has heard about. He even knows your thoughts. Yet still he values you. You are special! After all, he created you in his image.

Jesus pointed out the value of individual people a third time when he was speaking to the Pharisees:

'If you had a sheep that fell into a ditch on the Sabbath, wouldn't you lift it out? People are worth much more than sheep...' *(Matthew 12:11–12)*

Here's another rock on which to support your view of yourself:

Matthew 12:12
I am valuable to God.

You were created for a purpose

One of the basic questions everybody asks at some time in life is 'Why am I here?' Some part of us senses that we must be here for a purpose, that we have some kind of destiny. It's time to go back to that verse in Ephesians:

> For we are God's workmanship, created in Christ Jesus to do good works, which God prepared in advance for us to do. *(Ephesians 2:10)*

I didn't haphazardly drop off some kind of cosmic conveyor belt when I was created. Before I was born God had prepared a plan for my life.

Let your imagination loose for a moment...

The day of creation

As I lay on my bed, half asleep and half awake, I had a dream. I found myself present on Creation Day.

First I saw a jumbled heap on the floor – a pile of organs and limbs, eyes and skin, hair and bones. It was a peculiar sight. It was such a large pile too – I doubted whether all those parts could fit into one body.

As I looked, I saw the Creator begin his work. The pile of body parts seemed very small compared to him. Carefully and patiently he started fitting the pieces together, treating each as if it were a costly treasure – the small parts, the big parts, even the ugly parts that were made for the inside, though somehow these parts didn't look quite so ugly in his hands. Slowly the person began to take shape.

'Why did you make him this way?' I asked. 'Why not fatter or shorter, or taller? And what about his gifts and talents? How do you put *those* in?'

The Creator smiled and began to comment on his work as he continued.

'I will use these to listen to people who are hurting, who are in pain on the inside. He'll be good at that. Through him others will come to know that I care,' he said as he fixed on the ears.

Each part had a different function, but all were important. Everything fitted together perfectly, all to create this one living person. Finally the Creator stood his creation on his feet and gently breathed upon him. A shiver ran down my spine. The eyes slowly opened as life flooded in.

I watched in wonder, and I realised – I was looking at me.

Since my dream I've never thought of myself in quite the same way again.

The next rock on which to build is:

Ephesians 2:10
I have a purpose in life to do good.

You were specifically designed in advance for 'good works'. God didn't design you to be a failure in life. He made sure that you have the abilities you need to make a positive contribution to this world.

You're no loser
• • • • • • • • • • • • •

This all sounds very nice, you may be thinking, but it's not about me. I seem to bodge up everything I do.

Actually, to be in the position of reading this book, you have achieved something unbelievable against staggering odds...

Think for a few moments about a tiny capsule deep within your mother. Inside the capsule lies a minute egg, barely the size of a pinhead. Approximately half a million eggs entered this capsule at some stage but one was very special. This egg was catapulted out from the capsule into a long, straight tunnel filled with thick clear liquid. It began floating slowly downstream hoping to meet a partner. Otherwise it would die and share the fate of almost all the other eggs that had entered the capsule. Only a chosen few, hand-picked by God himself, survive this traumatic journey.

Turn your attention to another event. Inside your father a microscopic tadpole-like creature called a sperm lines up with another five hundred million sperm. A race is about to begin...

If you were to look closely at this sperm, you would discover that it is totally unique, containing its very own genetic code. Although a man produces billions of sperm (one thousand every second!), each one is different, no two are the same.

At this point your parents start to get a little bit interested in each other. In fact, they get pretty passionate. I know it's gross even to think about it, but it happens. They kiss, they touch, then – bang! The race is under way.

We'll pick up the race commentary inside your mother. Most of the five hundred million competing sperm have already dropped out of the marathon journey. Only the strongest and fittest survive. To reach the

egg, the remaining one hundred or so need to negoti-
ate the Fallopian tubes. Filled with hundreds of tiny
folds, the Fallopian tubes stand out like mountains in
the sperm's path. Many don't make it.

Other dangers lurk in this dangerous journey.
White blood cells, the violent security guards of the
body, ruthlessly attack and destroy any intruders entering their territory, including the sperm. The carnage is
terrible.

As well as bravery, this voyage requires pinpoint
accuracy without the assistance of maps, a compass or
any other navigational aid. A single wrong turn signals
the end for any sperm that strays from the path. Even
when the egg is in sight, some swim straight past to
their doom. To win this race you have to be pretty
smart too.

For the champion sperm to reach the egg, there is
one last struggle. Somehow it must get inside, and to
do this it starts smashing into the protective wall of the
egg, travelling as quickly, relatively speaking, as a
nuclear submarine. Its competitors do the same, and
there's a furious fight.

Finally the breakthrough occurs. The victor
emerges – it's in! Immediately a signal is sent to the
outer wall of the egg, and all other routes in are locked
down to prevent any other sperm from entering.

Inside the winner heads for its prize, moving like a
rotating drill as it cuts its way to the centre. There con-
ception occurs – and the miracle is complete.

This sperm is a true all-round champion. It has
achieved victory against incredible odds, overcoming
massive obstacles to its success. It is strong, brave, intelligent, fast and hardworking.

This is the story of an epic journey, a unique event
in history.

It's the story of how you were made.

A sense of awe and wonder at your body

In AD399 Augustine of Hippo, one of the greatest theologians of all time, wrote: 'People travel to wonder at the height of mountains, at the huge waves of the sea, at the long courses of rivers, at the vast compass of the ocean, at the circular motion of the stars, and they pass by themselves without wondering at all.'

> You are the one who put me together
> > inside my mother's body,
> and I praise you
> > because of the wonderful way you created me.
> Everything you do is marvellous!
> > Of this I have no doubt. *(Psalm 139:13–14)*

In this psalm we see someone pondering the incredible greatness of God. Suddenly he realises – God made him! Even when he was a few foetal cells in his mother's womb, God was there working on him. He knows he isn't an accident or a mere by-product of a chance evolutionary process. He has been lovingly created by a God whose works are described as 'wonderful'. God doesn't make any mistakes. What he creates is awesome.

Question

Do you regard yourself with that same sense of awe and wonder?

These words in the psalm are true of you too. Allow this truth to affect the way you see yourself. Instead of continually running yourself down, telling yourself you're worthless and a failure, believe what God says about you. God made you! This forms the next rock on which to build your view of yourself:

Psalm 139:14

I am awesomely and incredibly made.

Whatever others tell you, even if you think otherwise, you were no accident. Perhaps your parents said you were a mistake, that you weren't planned, but that isn't the truth. You may have come as a surprise to *them*, but you weren't a surprise to God. Before the world was created, he knew all about you and prepared a plan for your life. God doesn't make mistakes.

Question

What do you choose to believe – your feelings, what people say, or what God says?

For further amazing facts about your body, see the appendix at the end of the book.

5 WHAT LOVE IS THIS?

You may be thinking that all this stuff about being awesome and incredible sounds very flattering, but you can't quite connect it with – well – *you*! There's a perfectly good reason why you may feel like this. Remember I said we skipped out of Eden before things got nasty?

Sin
• • •
Adam and Eve are getting on fine with God, hanging out there in the garden. Great relationship. No worries.

Then another character enters the story. Not good news. It's the serpent...

He pulls a fast one on Eve, with the result that both Eve and Adam sour their friendship with God. They do the one thing God asked them not to do. It's not just a matter of pinching an apple – it's a wrong choice, an act of rebellion.

What makes them do it? They're greedy. They want to be like God. They decide they aren't going to submit any longer to their Creator. Who is he to tell them what to do? Surely they've been in the world long enough to take care of themselves.

THE RESULT
Like all wrong choices there are consequences. Adam and Eve no longer have a perfect relationship with

God. They have let him down badly, and he can't trust them any longer.

The perfect world God created is now messed up. Instead of relying on God and trusting him, Adam and Eve decide that they can make their own choices. The problem with us humans is that we are basically selfish and tend to put ourselves first. As you read on through Genesis, you see a trail of devastation. Jealousy, anger, sexual immorality, drunkenness, murder. Sin spreads like a computer virus, contaminating the world God made.

Well, you may be thinking, what's all this got to do with me? *I* wasn't there.

The problem is, you were! The Bible teaches that we are all 'in Adam' (see Romans 5). He represents every human being that has ever and will ever be created. So, in a real sense, *we* sinned when Adam sinned. If I had been there in the garden of Eden, I would have eaten the apple and so would you. As it was, sin entered into Adam and was passed on to all his descendants, like a hereditary disease.

HOW IT AFFECTS ME

Each of us is a curious combination. We are sinners (theological jargon for people who are infected by the spiritual disease of sin) *and* we are created in the image of God.

In the last few years the media has portrayed some fairly extreme examples of sin. In December 1995, headmaster Philip Lawrence was knifed to death by a teenager after coming to the rescue of a student who was being beaten up by a gang. In 1996 a fourteen-year-old girl was murdered by a group of her peers outside a fairground. And two-year-old Jamie Bulger was taken from his parents to a lonely railway line and beaten to death by two boys who hadn't even reached their teens. This is our dark side.

Most of us have never gone to such extremes. But what about nasty incidents like the one I saw recently at school? One of the Year 11 girls had brought in a T-shirt for all her friends to sign, as it was their last day at secondary school. One of her classmates, who was a bit of a bully, grabbed the T-shirt from her, rubbed it in mud and then proceeded to jump up and down on it. A crowd soon gathered and tried to provoke the two girls into fighting. Eventually the bully dumped the T-shirt into a bin and walked off. The Year 11 girl was left distraught.

We see evidence of sin in ourselves every day. It could be that we lie or that we're selfish. I see sin in myself when I drive my car. I hate being overtaken, and find myself accelerating to stop anyone going past me. Deep down I feel everyone else should just get out of my way!

However, though we are sinners we still bear the image of God. We don't resemble God perfectly any more, but you still see something of him in us. Every day I see young people help their friends cope with problems at home, or stick up for someone weaker who's being bullied. Many young people are involved in sponsored events to support the elderly, the homeless, people with learning disabilities, those suffering from cancer and other illnesses, and so on. Young people *do* care and can be incredibly loving.

Exercise

Take a moment to think of three things you have done recently to help other people. Write them here:

So good and evil live side by side in us. We can stick up for victims of bullying, help our friends deal with their problems, fight to the death for our families. Yet on the same day we can talk behind our friends' backs, take our parents for granted and get jealous of others around us.

The image of God and sin live and work together within each one of us.

The bad news

As well as teaching that we are all sinners, the Bible is quite clear that sin carries consequences. To understand why this is, look at it from God's perspective. He creates people to know him and to have a relationship with him. He creates the perfect world for them to live in so that they can enjoy life. He only gives them one rule to follow: don't touch the tree of the knowledge of good and evil. Apart from that, party on, dudes!

Then what? The one thing God asks man and woman not to do, they do. Worse than that, man and woman are now tainted with the one thing God cannot stand or tolerate – sin. God cannot stand sin because he is perfect holiness and perfect love. Here is an illustration that might help…

In the film *Liar, Liar*, Jim Carey plays a dodgy lawyer who will go to any lengths to win a case. Unfortunately for him, however, his son makes a birthday wish that makes it impossible for him to lie. Carey does everything possible to lie. He knows his career is doomed if he can't recover his old skill.

In one hilarious scene, he picks up a blue pen, and tries to say that it's a red pen. He struggles to get the words, 'This is a red pen', out of his mouth, but he can't. He attempts to write, 'This is a red pen', but that's impossible too. He ends up wrestling with the pen on the floor. However hard he tries, he can't call it a red pen, because the truth is it's blue. The scene ends with Carey getting up from the floor with the word 'blue' written all over his face.

In the same way, a holy and just God cannot sit back in his divine armchair and watch sin destroy the world he created. It is impossible for him to brush it under the carpet or hope it will go away.

We all have an innate sense of justice. We know, for example, that the Year 11 girl described just now was badly treated: the bully didn't deserve to get away with what she did. Likewise, when God sees the sin in our lives, it ought not to and cannot go unpunished.

And the Bible teaches that the ultimate consequence of sin in everyone's life is separation from God, which, since he is the source of life, means death.

TRAPPED

As a result of our sin, we are trapped on two counts. We can't stop sinning even if we want to. And, because of our sin, we deserve to be punished.

It doesn't matter that we try to live the perfect life, we find that we can't. Sin is in us, pulling us back, beating us down, actively controlling us. However many New Year's resolutions we make, there is no way we can be good enough to please God, though we may desperately want to. The apostle Paul put it this way:

> I don't understand why I act the way I do. I don't do what I know is right. I do the things I hate ... So I am not the one doing these evil things. The sin that lives in me is what does them. (Romans 7:15,17)

No matter how hard we try, we cannot break free from sin. It's not that we have been badly programmed genetically. If we don't take advantage of God's offer of freedom in Christ, sin works in us and controls us. We have no way of escape. We desperately need rescuing.

SLAVES

The Bible describes our condition as slavery. Listen to Jesus' conversation with some of the religious big cheeses. They ended up being rather offended by what he said:

> 'If you keep on obeying what I have said, you are truly my disciples. You will know the truth, and the truth will set you free.'
>
> They answered, 'We are Abraham's children! We have never been anyone's slaves. How can you say we will be set free?'
>
> Jesus replied, 'I tell you for certain that anyone who sins is a slave of sin!' *(John 8:31–34)*

Jesus told them they were trapped slaves and needed to be set free. This was a bit of a problem. The Jews knew that it was almost impossible for a slave to be set free. The only way was if he was *redeemed*. That's a bit of theological jargon, so let me explain.

Imagine you have got yourself into a spot of financial trouble. You find out how to use your parents' credit card and nip into town for a spree. After raiding Top Shop, HMV and Woollies you have the time of your life – until the monthly statement arrives through the post and your family is declared bankrupt.

A couple of thousand years ago, if this happened, the only way you would be able to pay off the debt would be to nip down to the local slave market on a Saturday afternoon and sell yourself. Someone likes the look of you and they buy you. The money goes to your family to pay off the debt, but you are now a slave and have to spend the rest of your life getting up at

4:30 in the morning and doing an all-day paper round for the local newsagent.

But what's all this about being redeemed?

If someone saw your pitiful condition and felt sorry for you, they could rescue you and send you back home to your groovy new wardrobe and CD collection. Say, for example, your mum had won a bit of money on the National Lottery, and her anger had subsided to the extent that she would consider having you back home, on the condition that you promise not to play your music after 11 o'clock at night. Your mum would need to approach your owner and make a business proposition. If your owner thought you were worth five grand (depending on how many copies of the Sun you had pushed through the locals' letterboxes before brekky), your mum would hand over the cash and you would have been redeemed or bought back. You would now be free to return home.

The good news
● ● ● ● ● ● ● ● ● ● ● ● ●

This history lesson is all very nice, you may be thinking, but what's it got to do with me? I've never had a paper round and my mum doesn't play the Lottery because she thinks it's gambling.

The Bible says:

> …you were not rescued by such things as silver or gold that don't last for ever. You were rescued by the precious blood of Christ… *(1 Peter 1:18–19)*

Remember, each of us is trapped in sin. We have no way of escape and because of it we deserve punishment. In other words, we are like slaves.

God saw each of us in this slavery to sin and, because he loved us, he wanted to rescue us, to set us free. He came down to the market-place with the readies in hand. He chose to buy us back to himself, because he created us as his children, to know him and to have a relationship with him.

The price he paid wasn't five thousand pounds or ten thousand pounds. The verse above tells us that God purchased us with the precious blood of Christ. The expression 'the blood of Christ' refers to the fact that Jesus gave his life and died on a cross for us.

THE CROSS

But why did Jesus have to die? This brings us to our second point. We mentioned that God is holy and just. He cannot turn a blind eye to sin, which deserves punishment. But instead of punishing us God allowed his Son to die on the cross, and in dying he took our punishment on our behalf. Jesus wasn't dying for his own sins, but for ours. This way, God could both punish sin and rescue us. The cross satisfied the need for sin to be punished *and* it enabled us to be set free.

THE COST

In a small village in Wales there is a plaque placed near the foot of a hill in remembrance of an outstanding act of love many years ago. The village was built around a coalmine dug deep into the hill. In order to get to work, the miners had to board a minibus and drive up the hill along a narrow, curving path. They were dropped off at the top and the finishing shift was taken back down the hill in the same vehicle.

On one such trip down, the minibus was packed with tired, grubby miners who had just completed a shift. As they journeyed down the hill the brakes failed, and the minibus went hurtling along the twisted, narrow path. With great skill the driver somehow managed to keep it from careering over the edge and down the hillside.

As the minibus neared safety and turned a steep bend, the driver saw a young boy on a bicycle riding straight towards them. In that split second he was faced with a choice. He could either swerve off the road and down the hillside, almost certainly killing all the men in the minibus. Or he could keep going and run straight into the small boy on the bicycle.

In that moment he decided to keep going. The little boy died instantly.

Afterwards, when the minibus came to a halt, the men were furious with the driver. 'How could you do that? He was just a boy. You should have driven off the road and risked killing us.'

The driver turned to them with tears streaming down his face. 'That boy...' he stammered brokenly, 'was my son...'

✝

On the cross God chose to take the life of his Son, Jesus, so that we could be saved and enjoy eternal life.

BUT WHY?

Jason Tuskes was a seventeen-year-old student and an expert swimmer with a passion for scuba diving. He loved his family very much, his mother, his wheelchair-bound father and also his brother, Christian.

One Tuesday morning he kissed his mother on the cheek and headed off on an expedition to explore a series of underwater caves in Florida. He said he wouldn't be too long as he planned to rejoin the family that evening to celebrate his mother's birthday with the rest of the family.

While Jason was exploring the caves, he realised he was lost. His anxiety led to panic and he ended up wedging himself tightly in a narrow underwater passageway.

Aware that he was completely trapped, he reached down for his diver's knife and his yellow air-tank which was slowly running out of oxygen. He used his knife as a pen and scratched a message into the metal tank: 'I love you, Mum, Dad and Christian. I always have and I always will.'

Shortly afterwards, the air ran out and he died.

His parents were overwhelmed to think that Jason had thought of them in his final moments of life. It communicated something very special to them.

Likewise, Jesus communicated something to us through his death. His message is etched blood red on a Roman cross, and it says, 'I love you. I always have and I always will.'*

> 'God loved the people of this world so much that he gave his only Son, so that everyone who has faith in him will have eternal life and never really die. God did not send his Son into the world to condemn its people. He sent him to save them!' (John 3:16–17)

In short

The rock on which to build our view of ourselves is:

John 3:16

I am loved by God.

Note

* From 'You're worth dying for', Rubell Shelley. Used by permission.

6 YOU'RE THE CHILD OF A KING

The Disney film *The Lion King* is set in the African plains, in an area known as the Pride Lands. The story centres around Simba, the young son of the powerful king of the Pride Lands, Mufasa. Mufasa is a good king and respected by all his subjects except his own brother, Scar, who is jealous and hungry for power.

Scar hates Mufasa and seeks to kill him so that he can become king. He manages to achieve this by arranging for a stampede of buffalo to run through a deep gorge where Simba is playing. As soon as Mufasa hears that his beloved son is in danger, he bravely risks his own life by running into the middle of the stampede to rescue him. He manages to save his son, but loses his own life as he is crushed to death in the stampede.

As Simba lies crying over his father's body, his evil uncle Scar arrives and tells Simba that it was his fault his father died. He advises Simba to run away so that others don't hear of what he has done. Frightened and scared, Simba runs away from the Pride Lands, and Scar becomes the new king.

Several years later, when Simba is fully grown, he is playing in the jungle many miles from his real home with his new friends, Pumba and Timone. As they play, a lioness attacks Pumba and Timone. But Simba comes to their aid. As he struggles with the lioness, he discovers that it is his childhood friend from the Pride Lands.

She tells him what has happened there under Scar's rule. The kingdom is now in ruins, there is no food or water, and everyone is starving. She begs Simba to return, as he is the only one who can save them.

But Simba refuses. He blames himself for his father's death. Besides, he doesn't feel that he is strong and brave like his father. He may look strong and brave on the outside, but inside he feels weak and scared.

Then Simba meets Raficki, the wise monkey, who knew his father. When Simba asks the monkey, 'Who are you?', Raficki replies, 'The question is, who are *you?*'

Raficki takes Simba to a pool and tells him that if he looks closely into it, he will see how his father lives on in him.

Simba looks at his reflection and begins to see his father's likeness. He sees a vision and hears his father's voice saying, 'You have forgotten who you are … You are more than what you have become. Remember who you are. You are my son … Remember who you are. Remember, remember…'

Simba realises his true identity. He is the son of a powerful king, but he had forgotten this. Discovering his true identity brings a powerful change in his life. He starts to feel like a king, and he bravely returns to the Pride Lands and overthrows Scar.

Becoming a Christian involves a change in identity. It doesn't just change what you do, it changes who you are. It brings you into a new relationship with God. You recognise that he is your Father, and you become more fully aware that you are his much loved child. *This is who you really are!* It's one of the most important discoveries you can make.

I want you

I'm sure you can remember participating in games where you were asked to line up and wait to be picked by the team captains. It can be a pretty horrific experience. Imagine the queue narrowing down to nearly nothing, and still no one seems to want you on their team. To be last would be humiliating enough, but if one of the captains then looked at you disdainfully and said to the other, 'You can have…', you would be left feeling majorly inadequate.

> Before the world was created, God had Christ choose us to live with him and to be his holy and innocent and loving people. God was kind and decided that Christ would choose us to be God's own adopted children. *(Ephesians 1:4–5)*

What this verse is saying is that God selected you. He picked you out and said, 'I want him on my side.' And he doesn't just pick us to play in his team. It's far more personal than that. He picks us to join his family.

> God's Spirit doesn't make us slaves who are afraid of him. Instead, we become his children and call him our Father. God's Spirit makes us sure that we are his children. *(Romans 8:15–16)*

When we become Christians and God buys us back to himself, he doesn't make us into slaves who are afraid of a cruel master. The Holy Spirit comes into our lives and lets us know that our new boss is actually our father, and we have been adopted as his children.

To understand what it means to be adopted, it might be helpful to return for a moment to the first century…

Roman culture was well-known for its attitude towards sex. Basically, anything went. The wealthy frequently had mistresses or slept with prostitutes, fathering numerous children. Women who were too poor to bring up their children on their own were forced to abandon them in the street.

The only hope was if the mother went to the wealthy man's home and presented the baby to him. The Roman lord would then choose whether or not to take care of the child and allow them to live in his house. If he gave the thumbs-down sign, it meant he wasn't prepared to do this, and the child would almost certainly end up on the street. A thumbs-up meant he had chosen to keep the child and provide for them.

Imagine. When God saw you, he looked at you, smiled and gave a double thumbs-up! He wanted you, he chose you, he has adopted you.

This provides us with another couple of rocks on which to base our self-worth:

Ephesians 1:5
I have been chosen by God and adopted into his family.

Romans 8:15-16
I am God's child. He is my dad.

Why has God got such big hands?

One preacher I heard talking on this subject said that God has got a picture of you in his wallet. Every now and again, he takes it out and says to one of the angels, 'That's my son. Great, isn't he?' Or 'See her? She's my daughter – she's really special.'

When I heard this I thought, How awesome. But later I went to Bible college where they teach you to think for yourself and ask deep theological questions. I started questioning everything, like 'Has God *really* got a picture of me in his wallet? Has God *got* a wallet? Why would God need a wallet anyway?'

I decided God didn't need a wallet, so he probably didn't have one. The logical conclusion was that he didn't have a picture of me on him wherever he went. Sad really. But hang on…

In one of our lectures I came across a verse buried deep in the book of Isaiah. It said that God could hold the oceans of the earth in the palm of his hands (Isaiah 40:12). Wow! I can hold about a quarter of a cup of water in the palm of my hands, and even then it leaks out. But God can hold the Pacific Ocean in his.

Then I begin to think (as you do), 'Why does God have such big hands?' (Can you see how Bible college can do strange things to your mind?) Soon I found the answer to my question in the same Bible book:

> Can a mother forget the baby at her breast
>   and have no compassion on the child she has
>   borne?
> Though she may forget,
>   I will not forget you!
> See, I have engraved you on the palms of my
>   hands… *(Isaiah 49:15–16)*

God doesn't just have a picture of me in his wallet. It's even better than that. He's got a picture of me engraved on his hand! He's crazy about me!

Of course, these are illustrations of the truth, pictures to help us grasp something of how much God loves us. If it helps you to think of the picture in the wallet or the engraving, go right ahead. The next rock:

Isaiah 49:16

I am engraved on the palm of God's hands.

Our image of God

Maybe you're thinking, Hang on. This doesn't really tie up with the way *I* think of God. We all imagine God in a certain way, and maybe the picture of God loving you is hard for you to relate to.

Perhaps your picture of a father is not particularly positive. Your own father may have hurt you, physically, emotionally or sexually. Perhaps you never even knew your father, and the picture you have of a father is someone who is never there when you need them, someone who lets you down or rejects you. Some fathers show very little interest in their children; they always appear too busy or concerned with other more important issues to have time for their kids. There's also the kind of father who has incredibly high expectations, who makes his kids feel they are never good enough.

Before we move on to the next chapter, where we

will look more closely at the type of father God is, take
a moment to answer the following:

Exercise

How does your experience of your earthly father
affect the way you see God?

Jot down your thoughts on what you would consider to be the qualities of the perfect human father.

Does God possess these qualities?

7 THE SORT OF FATHER GOD IS

Happy families?

I'm sure you've heard this story about the man with two sons. One was a bit wild, the other was – well – a bit stuck up. The wild one got in a strop one day and gave his dad a mouthful.

'I'm sick of living out here in the sticks, and I'm sick of living with you. You know when you die I'll get loads of dosh. Well, I don't want to hang around that long. Give me the money now – I'm outa here!'

His dad gave him the money and off he went.

He had read about the club scene on the Med so he got on a plane and headed for the sun. It didn't take him long to blow all his cash on booze, drugs and the local ladies. Soon he was skint.

Just about this time, a recession crippled the local economy and unemployment soared. Here the son was, in a foreign country, with no friends (his new mates had all made themselves scarce when his money ran out), no cash and no way of supporting himself. He looked for a job but there was nothing going. Finally, in absolute desperation, he ended up on a pig farm back in the sticks (he *hated* the countryside!). He was so broke he couldn't even scrape together enough money for a burger at the Greasy Spoon over the road. When no one was looking, he grabbed a handful of the food he fed to the pigs.

'Am I thick or what?' he thought to himself. 'Here I am up to my eyeballs in pig manure and starving to death. The workers on my dad's farm have a better life than me. I've got to get back – I'll die if I don't!

'But what am I going to say to Dad?'

He thought long and hard about this.

'I suppose I'd better be honest. I know – I'll say, "I'm sorry, Dad, I really blew it this time. I'm sorry for hurting you, and I don't expect you to treat me like your son any more. But at least I can work hard on the farm and pay back some of the cash I got from you."'

Anxiously going over his speech in his mind, he set off for home, walking or hitching lifts on passing fishing boats, lorries, vans… Eventually he was set down, dirty and tired, at the front gate of his home. He made his way up the path and raised his hand to ring the doorbell. But, before he could push the bell, the door flew open. There waiting in the doorway was his dad.

He began to trot out his speech. 'I'm sorry, Dad. I've been a complete idiot. I let you down, I…'

He was rudely interrupted. 'This is incredible! I thought you were dead! This is the best day of my life! You're back and you're OK. Come on in!'

His father pulled him into the house.

'Here's a little welcome-home present – a ring. And why not go up and put on some fresh clothes? I got you some new ones. While you're doing that I'll get on the phone to the Indian and order up a rajah's feast. Then I'll invite everyone round tonight – we'll have a party.'

As the son headed upstairs to have his first bath in months, his father looked up lovingly after him. 'This is a great day, son. I thought I'd lost you. I'm so glad you're back!'

More than any story in the Bible, this one in Luke 15:11–24 Steve Mawston translation above) illustrates how your Father in heaven feels about you.

Jesus told this story, and he didn't mean it as a 'then they all lived happily ever after' sort of story. Or as a yarn about what experts call a dysfunctional family. In fact, it has very little to do with your everyday Joneses down the road. Jesus wasn't talking about an earthly relationship at all, but about a heavenly one. God is the father, each one of us is the stroppy, rebellious child.

On the surface, the story is about a headstrong young man who makes a major mistake. Underneath, it is about how much our Father in heaven loves his children. God is willing to accept anyone who comes to him, whatever we have been up to, however much of a mess we have made of our lives. His eyes see beyond our grubby faults and failings. His arms are always open, inviting us to enter his embrace and experience his Father-heart of love.

He doesn't just accept us: he accepts us joyfully (see verses 22–24). There are no preconditions. We don't need to make up for our mistakes, pay him back or try to get into his good books.

Your Father in heaven will accept you if you turn to him, because he loves you unconditionally.

Love is forgiving.
Love is for giving.
It is a gift.
It is not deserved.
A gift can only be received
    or rejected.
Will you accept or reject
God's forgiveness
    offered freely
    as a gift

**from God
to you
with love?**

You've got to love this rock!

~~~~~~

Luke 15:11-24
**I am accepted and loved unconditionally by Father
God.**

~~~~~~

THE FORGIVING FATHER

The story of the lost son is a story of forgiveness. When
the sinful son returns, the father doesn't ground him,
throw a wobbly, ignore him or make him do the dishes
for a month.

He forgives him.

Perhaps there are things you have done that you
feel are simply too big to be forgiven.

'Will God forgive me if I've lost my virginity and
I'm not married? Does he still love me?'

Yes!

'Will God forgive me if I get stoned at a party with
my mates?'

Yes!

All you have to do is what the lost son did in the
story. Come back to your Father and say, 'I'm sorry, I
messed up.' The Bible calls this confessing your sins.

The principal at London Bible College mes-
merised us practising preachers in one chapel service
with a story about how hard it is to accept forgiveness.

In the 1984 Olympic Games in Los Angeles, the American women's 4 x 400 metres relay team made it to the final. The race took place on the last day of the Games. The stadium was packed. The crowd cheered wildly for every American competitor.

The race began and the American team went into the lead. The first runner handed the baton to the second member of the squad who ran an excellent leg. As she finished her lap, she was still in the lead and she reached forward to hand the baton to the third runner. Somehow they got their timing mixed up and the baton fell to the ground. The crowd gasped. Two other teams passed the American runner. She bent down, picked up the baton and started to sprint again. She was in third place, and the team still had a chance of winning the gold medal.

Then, for some reason, the third runner slowed down and stepped off the track. The camera switched to the face of the second runner who stared in disbelief. What was the girl doing? Why had she stopped?

The problem was that the third runner thought that if you dropped the baton, you were out of the race.

𝒳 𝒳 𝒳

The Christian life is often likened to a race (see Galatians 5:7, NIV). Sometimes we run well, sometimes we run badly. Along the way we make mistakes, we drop the baton. But the good news is that *all is not lost*! We're *not* out of the race!

> If we confess our sins to God, he can always be trusted to forgive us and take our sins away. (1 John 1:9)

So if you've got into stuff you know deep down you shouldn't have got into, go to God and confess it. Say,

'Sorry'. He will forgive you! Then you can stand firm on the next rock:

---

1 John 1:9
I am forgiven by God.

THE FORGETFUL FATHER

Sometimes this forgiveness lark sounds too good to be true. Wouldn't it be great to have human parents like that? We find it hard to accept that God loves us this way. We're waiting for the catch, the angry outburst, the stony silence, the delayed rebuke.

Parents can go on about things for months. Every time you get into the tiniest bit of trouble, reference is made to your previous shortcomings. 'He's always in trouble, our Steven. You'd think he'd learn, but no. If I've told him once, I've told him a thousand times...' Sound familiar?

Not only does God forgive us, he forgets our sins too. He doesn't keep bringing them up, reminding us of what we have done in the past. They are gone, past, over with, remembered no more.

Writer Corrie ten Boom has said that God throws our sin into the middle of a lake and puts up a sign saying, 'No fishing'. Other people may try to remind us and point the finger at us. Even the devil will try to whisper reminders in your ear of what you've done. But God forgives and forgets. Once you have confessed your sin, he highlights whatever you did on his multimedia computer and presses 'Delete'. A little box appears on his monitor saying 'Are you sure you want to delete wotsisname's sin?' and he types, 'Yes.' From then on it's gone, irretrievably.

A FATHER WHO DOESN'T CONDEMN

Often we aren't as good at forgiving ourselves as God is. We give ourselves a hard time, tell ourselves we're not good enough to be a Christian, and end up feeling totally beaten up spiritually. We don't think we are forgiven because we don't *feel* forgiven. Small everyday incidents – meeting a certain person, hearing a sermon or visiting a particular place – all trigger memories of what we did in the past. We relive it in our minds and end up feeling as bad as we did when we first sinned.

This kind of condemnation does not come from God. He promised to forgive you if you have confessed your sin and said sorry. To go back on his promise would make him both a liar (because he promised to forgive you) and a not-very-nice-person.

If you're experiencing condemnation, it's probably coming from one of three sources:

- From inside you.
- From another person who is trying to make you feel guilty.
- From Satan who is having a go at you. (Don't worry, the chapter on 'Changing the tapes' will help you sort him out.)

God loves you, accepts you and forgives you.

> There is now no condemnation for those who are in Christ Jesus. *(Romans 8:1)*

If God is your Father and you are living for him, the following rock is one you can depend on:

Romans 8:1

I am free from guilt and condemnation.

'HELLO, THIS IS GOD. I'D LIKE TO SPEAK TO…'
The more you learn about God, the more you realise how much he wants to have a relationship with us. It's almost as if God would go to any lengths to get to know us and to get us to know him. That's why he's not into condemning people and making them feel guilty all the time. Think of someone you know who always seems to be putting you down, trying to make you feel small. You just *love* spending time with them – I don't think.

God is committed to building intimate personal relationships with people. For example, when his disciples asked him to teach them to pray, Jesus taught them to call God 'Father' (Matthew 6:9).

The way you address a person says something about the type of relationship you have with that person. For example, when my bank manager writes to me or telephones me, he calls me 'Mr Mawston'. When I was at school, my headmaster used to call me 'Mawston'. Neither of these two people knew me very well. Those who have closer relationships with me call me 'Steven'. My old form teacher used to call me this. But my friends call me 'Steve'. They know that I prefer 'Steve' to 'Steven'. And the people who know me best, my closest friends and my wife, call me 'Ste'.

You see, the more personal the relationship people have with me, the more personal the name they use.

Imagine what it would be like if my wife referred to me as 'Mr Mawston' all the time.

'Mr Mawston, I'm home.'

'Mr Mawston, shall we do the shopping tonight?'

'Mr Mawston, I love you.'

Likewise, in our relationship with God we don't have to address him as 'Our most beneficent Almighty Suzerain, Creator and Lord…' Instead, Jesus taught us to call him 'Father'.

The passage in Romans that we looked at earlier tells us that we can use an even more intimate expression to talk to God:

> For you did not receive a spirit that makes you a slave again to fear, but you received the Spirit of sonship. And by him we cry, 'Abba, Father.' *(Romans 8:15)*

We can call God 'Abba'. This isn't just the name of a seventies Swedish pop group: it's an Aramaic word which literally means 'Daddy', the word used by a child to address their father. It tells us that we can have an intimate loving relationship with our Father in heaven.

LOVE IS SPELT T.I.M.E.

God is not a grumpy, tired-out father who comes in from work, puts his feet up in front of the telly and stays there until bedtime, giving out 'do not disturb' vibes. He values each of his children and is interested in the smallest details of our lives. Nothing is too trivial to bring to him, and we don't have to compete for his attention. He listens and hears us all the time, particularly when we are going through a rough patch.

God never ignores you or looks straight through you as if you're invisible. He is listening when we need to talk about stuff that's bugging us, and he is very good at keeping things confidential. He hears and understands. Nothing shocks him. It's great to know he is always there.

YOUR FATHER IN HEAVEN LOVES YOU AS YOU ARE

Babies have always fascinated me. Watch any parent with a newborn child and you will catch a glimpse of what love is. I mean, let's face it, most newborn babies aren't oil paintings. When a parent presents their off-spring to you proudly, you are in a fairly delicate situation. If you said what you really thought, it would probably be something like, 'What did you name Shorty with the funny-shaped face then?'

Instead, most of us smile approvingly and say, 'Awww, isn't she/he cute!'

Unfortunately it's not always easy to tell whether a baby is male or female. I've lost count of the number of dirty looks I've had from parents because I've said 'Isn't he gorgeous' when 'he' was actually a 'she'. It's safer simply to smile and say nothing intelligible. An 'Awww' is sufficient.

The point is that, despite their looks, newborn babies are still loved.

It's not as if babies do anything to earn your love either. You can't say to a one-month-old baby, 'Do us a favour, mate. Make us a plate of chips for my tea.' Or 'Will you finish the clearing-up for us while I nip out down the park?'

On the contrary, babies can be a real pain. If you or I behaved the same way as a typical sprog, we would be in serious trouble. If you get the munchies, maybe you go to the kitchen and help yourself to a packet of crisps or a handful of biscuits? Yeah? You don't start bawling and squawking at the top of your lungs, and wait for someone to come along and feed you.

Babies don't earn love by what they do, by being good at hoovering or because they've got the highest grades in class. Babies don't merit love: they haven't done anything to deserve it. Their only experience of love is unconditional. They are loved simply for *who they are*. That's what this chapter is really all about.

Love with no strings attached

As we grow older, from childhood into adolescence and from adolescence to adulthood, we enter a world where we are often no longer treated unconditionally as if we are of worth and value. We enter a world where, by and large, acceptance and love have to be earned.

When we go to school we discover that love – or perhaps it would be more appropriate to say popularity and approval – tends to be dependent on the things we do. To maximise the amount of love we receive, we may need to score high marks in tests, behave impeccably, excel in sports… If we fail in any of these areas, we may encounter a certain amount of hostility from teachers or parents. The message often seems to be 'Do better and I'll love you more'.

Soon our peers join in. We have to dress in a certain way, we need to hang out with the right people, wear the right brand of trainers, listen to the right music. We are no longer accepted unconditionally for just being *who we are*. Now there are strings attached and conditions to be met.

'I WANT TO KNOW WHAT LOVE IS…'
To escape this world, we might try to retreat, to hide away. But as soon as we switch on the TV, another set of qualifications appears. (Remember, we looked at these in the section on the media in chapter two?)

The fact is that as teenagers our experience of love is conditional. It is not surprising that we sometimes long to go back to the childhood world in which we were valued and appreciated with no strings attached.

I'm lying in bed, dreaming about playing basketball in front of thousands of screaming fans. The scores are tied with ten seconds left on the clock. You could cut the tension with a knife as the seconds tick away. The ball is in my hands, and I'm standing well outside the three-point zone. I rise into the air to take a jumpshot. The ball travels towards the basket in slow motion. Everyone waits, holding their breath. As the last second ticks away – swish! – the ball flies into the basket without even touching the sides. The crowd go ballistic. The team hoist me onto their shoulders to do a lap of honour. My name is being chanted by thousands of adoring fans...

Why do we have dreams like this? Because we all want to be deeply loved, and somehow we feel that to earn this kind of love we need to do something outstanding. Our problem is that we base our sense of worth on all the wrong conditions: what our parents think, what our friends think, how we perform.

But if we understood the type of love God has for us, it would bring us such incredible security. Somehow other people's views of us don't matter so much because you know God thinks you're amazing. It's as if you're his only child, and he loves you with a perfect love. You no longer need to live up to a set of expectations. The fact that you bodge up your mocks isn't going to mean that he loves you any the less. He cannot love you any more than he does already.

This kind of love is our deepest human need. The problem is, we look to other people to satisfy it. But however wonderful your mum/dad/gran/grandad/boyfriend/girlfriend is, however much they praise and affirm you, they can never provide *the answer*. This kind of love cannot be found in any human relationship – human beings are just too imperfect. This is why it's so important that you build your self-worth on what God thinks of you.

He loves us because he created us. He loves us because he sent his Son to die for us. We learn of his love through our relationship with him.

So far we've quarried some great stuff to build on.

8 IN YOUR HEART AS WELL AS YOUR HEAD

I was brought up to be a Jehovah's Witness. When I was about five, my mum had a nervous breakdown. At the time my father was a very heavy drinker, and when Mum recovered she and my dad didn't get on. When I was six my father abused me. I kept quiet and believed him when he said, 'All daddies do this.' A year later he raped me.

In some ways, when my parents split up, I was lucky because at least the things that had been happening with Dad stopped. Nobody knew what he had done to me. It wasn't until I was twelve and had sex education at school that I realised what had happened was wrong.

At that time in my life, even though I was young, I had learned not to discuss my feelings. I was always scared of being laughed at. I threw myself into the Jehovah's Witness Organisation, but I never felt happy with who I was, in fact I hated being me. At night in bed I'd pretend to be someone else. It was the only way I could get to sleep.

When I was fourteen, I realised that being a Jehovah's Witness was only making things worse. I turned to men thinking they could give me what I needed – acceptance and love. All I got was loneliness, feeling used and feeling dirty. I know now I was acting this way because I was trying to escape from my emotions. I thought that I was a failure, that there was nothing good about me. I got so low, I tried to take my own life – and got frustrated because I couldn't even manage to do that.

It was just before I tried to take my life that I met a Christian worker at school. At first I found it hard to discuss my feelings or even to look him in the eye.

As the months went by, I slowly began to trust him. I saw a difference in him and in his friends who were Christians. They cared, they wanted to give. They weren't just out for what they could get. What really hit home was the amount of time they spent telling me I was of worth as a person. Nobody had ever really taken the time to listen and understand.

I started going to church and loved the atmosphere, the way people were always glad to see you. Although I felt better in myself, the problems were far from over. I was taken into care when I was fifteen. I had tried to be a Christian, but I wasn't. I was wishy-washy and, at the slightest problem, I would stop going to church. I was hooked on men, maybe because I'd never been accepted by my dad. I was looking for someone to fill his shoes.

I carried on going to church, then leaving and coming back again. A few months ago (I am now 17), I was meeting with a young woman from the church for Bible study. One night she persuaded me to go to the youth meeting. I agreed to go just to keep her quiet.

I sat and listened to the preaching, and it struck a chord in me. Before I knew it, the speaker had finished and was asking if anyone had drifted away from Jesus. I didn't realise what I was doing until I noticed my hand was in the air. I went to the front and he prayed for me. That night the Holy Spirit moved on me. It was the most beautiful experience of my life.

I still had massive problems related to my dad. At night I would see his face in my room and feel his hands reaching out to me. As the Holy Spirit touched me, I had brief glimpses of what Dad had done to me. But instead of feeling frightened and upset, I felt calm, maybe even detached in a sense. When I came out of it, I felt so loved, so cared for. It was as if I was being told that I'd be okay now. The past which had caused me so much pain and heartache was just that – in the past. The years of tears and bitterness were over. All that mattered now was my future and what I would do with it. That evening I decided what had happened was no coincidence. I couldn't have made myself feel so calm about something that had caused so much pain. I knew from then on there was only one way to live, and that was for Jesus.

Things have improved for me, though they aren't always easy. Being a Christian never is, and there are many other pathways which seem less demanding. But in the long run they cause so much pain and unhappiness. I feel secure in the love I've found in Jesus. I'm sure he's the only way.

This moving story was written by a courageous young woman who has been through things most of us will never know, and who has had to deal with powerful feelings as a result. She is struggling with many issues, but God is changing her by his love.

'It's better felt than telt'

On several occasions I've been involved with young people who have started to search for a missing parent after years of separation. At times like these it would have been little comfort for me to say, 'I tell you what. I'll go and meet your dad (whom you haven't seen since you were two). You stay here and carry on with your school work. I'll come back and tell you exactly what he's like. That way you'll get to know him.' How do you think a young person would have felt if I'd adopted this approach?

You only get to know someone by having a relationship with them. You could describe someone very close to you, someone who loves you and whom you love. It could be your boyfriend or girlfriend or a parent. You could describe them in great detail: their height, weight, figure, the colour of their eyes and hair, their personality, likes and dislikes. You could tell me about their dreams for the future, and about their past. But no matter how well you described them to me, I still wouldn't know them. Why? Because to really know a person you need to encounter them, have a relationship with them. It's to do with your heart as well as your head.

Similarly, it's no good me just writing two chapters about how much God loves you. It's helpful to some degree, but if all it does is remain intellectual knowledge, it's not going to affect you very much. You need to get to know God for yourself.

It's one thing to know in your head that God loves you. It's another thing to know deep down that he loves you and to experience his love. 'It's better felt than telt', as one old lady in our church used to say.

YES, BUT HOW?

The first Christians had a hard time grasping God's love. When the apostle Paul wrote a letter to a large church in Ephesus, he prayed that everyone in the church there would be strengthened 'with power through his Spirit' so that they would be able to grasp 'how wide and long and high and deep is the love of Christ, and to know this love that surpasses knowledge...' (Ephesians 3:16–19).

Paul is telling the Ephesian Christians that they need the Holy Spirit's power to help them understand how incredible God's love is. This love surpasses, or is beyond, knowledge. Even if you get ten A stars in your GCSE's and four A levels, you still can't understand with your mind how wide and deep and long and wide is the love God has for you. Only the Holy Spirit can show you how much he loves you.

OK, you may be thinking, I need to know God's love in my heart as well as my head, and the only way I can do this is through the Holy Spirit. But I get so confused about the Holy Spirit. I wish someone could explain it all to me clearly.

Well, here goes...

The Holy Spirit – what or who?

First, the Holy Spirit is a person: he isn't some mysterious force, like electricity. I used to think of him that way, that he was a kind of spiritual energy which zapped people causing a sort of Ready-Brek glow to encompass them. But the Holy Spirit isn't a force or an 'it'.

He has feelings. The Bible says, 'Do not grieve the Holy Spirit.' The fact that the Holy Spirit can be grieved shows he is a person.

And the Holy Spirit can think and speak. I remember one Monday morning when I was sitting in my office and a student I was meant to see hadn't turned up. The previous day I'd been in church, listening to someone talk about being led by the Spirit. The preacher explained that God doesn't give us a map with precise directions to travel through life. Instead, he gives us a real life guide – the Holy Spirit. OK, I thought to myself, now's the time to see if what he was talking about was kosher.

So I sat in my office and asked God to show me who I should talk to during period 1. Then I listened.

I didn't hear a loud voice over the school tannoy system (probably because we don't have one). But I did hear something like a voice in my mind, speaking to me. (Don't worry – this is a thoroughly biblical concept. Jesus himself was led by the Holy Spirit – see Luke 4:1.)

The person whose name came into my mind was Vicky. Vicky was a girl I'd talked to a few times because she was a victim of bullying. I felt the Holy Spirit was telling me to go and see her. So I dug out her timetable and went down to her class.

The lesson hadn't begun. Vicky was lined up in the corridor waiting to go into English.

'Vicky,' I shouted, 'the Holy Spirit has told me to come and minister to you!'

Actually, that's *not* what I said. Sounds pretty spiritual, doesn't it? But it would have totally freaked her out, and I wouldn't like to think what it would have done to her credibility (or mine) with the rest of the class. In fact, all I did was ask her to come up to my room. As we walked up the stairs, I enquired how things were going.

'Funny you should ask,' she said. 'On the way to school today I got beaten up by Michelle. I was going to come and see you but I was too scared in case she found out.' We talked for a few minutes and were able to get some things sorted out.

This is just one illustration of how the Holy Spirit can guide or lead you. For example, if you've got a big decision like your options, or whether to stay on at Sixth Form or go to college, then make sure you pray first and ask God to show you what to do. Sometimes he speaks, as he did to me about Vicky. At other times he leaves it up to you to make the decision. After all, he did give you an incredible mind (see the appendix at the end of this book). And sometimes he speaks to you through the Bible. A particular verse you are reading will seem especially important or relevant for the situation you're in. This is the Holy Spirit drawing it to your attention.

e

The Holy Spirit is a gift from the Father. Before Jesus left earth to return to heaven, he told his distraught disciples, 'I will ask the Father to send you the Holy Spirit who will help you and always be with you. The Spirit will show you what is true' (John 14:16–17).

You cannot earn a gift. If your uncle offers you a birthday present, you don't say, 'Cheers, I'll come round every Monday night and wash your car. Once I've done that for a month, then I'll deserve it.' You can't earn a gift, you can only receive it.

The Holy Spirit isn't just for people who are mega-spiritual. You don't have to read the Bible for three hours a day, or stand up and give your testimony every week in RE, to earn the Holy Spirit. You can't do anything to earn the Holy Spirit. All you can do is ask the Father and he will give him to you (see Luke 11:9–13).

The type of gift a person gives to another person tells you how they feel about them. For example, at Christmas time my aunts would get me pyjamas and socks every year, bless them. I mean, don't get me wrong, they were great gifts. I just wasn't a pyjama-and-socks sort of person.

My parents, however, were all-round champions when it came to present buying. Not only did they spend wads of cash, but they seemed to be divinely inspired. (Either that or they scraped around in the fireplace for the list I left Santa.) When I got gifts from them, I felt appreciated and loved – and had a lot of fun too, it must be said.

God gave us the most awesome gift – the Holy Spirit. He didn't give us some second-hand cast-off. He gave us a gift that helps us cope with life and affirms that we are of worth and value in his sight.

CHILL OUT

A lot of young people get scared of the Holy Spirit. Jesus obviously anticipated this, because he had a lengthy chat with his disciples to make sure they wouldn't be frightened.

> 'Which one of you fathers would give your hungry child a snake if the child asked for a fish? Which one of you would give your child a scorpion if the child asked for an egg? As bad as you are, you still know how to give good gifts to your children. But your heavenly Father is even more ready to give the Holy Spirit to anyone who asks.' (Luke 11:11–13)

If you asked your dad for some fish and chips for lunch, he wouldn't nip down to the local pet shop on the way back from the chippie and slip a rattlesnake under your chips. Likewise, if you asked him for a boiled egg for breakfast, would he slip a scorpion in with your soldiers (the bits of bread you dip in your egg)? Well, if your imperfect earthly parents wouldn't do that, it's even less likely God would give you something to hurt you. He loves you.

Now that we know who the Holy Spirit is, the next question is…

What does he do?

• • • • • • • • • • • • • • • •

Some words on the subject from Jesus. He is just about to finish the job he'd come to do on earth and head home (much to the disciples' displeasure):

> 'I will ask the Father, and he will give you another Counsellor to be with you forever – the Spirit of truth.' *(John 14:16–17)*

'ANOTHER COUNSELLOR'

Jesus was the first Counsellor. The second Counsellor, the Holy Spirit, is different only in the sense that you can't see him. He comes into your life when you become a Christian. He comes to live in you, but he does the same kind of stuff that Jesus did when he was on earth.

Quick brainstorm

Write down here some of the qualites you think a really good counsellor would have.

I think a good counsellor is a good listener who understands where you're coming from.

In school we have a group of peer counsellors who help other students who have problems. They're great because they are the same age and facing similar challenges. So when students talk to a peer counsellor, they feel they are talking to someone who understands. A counsellor should also help people cope better with what they are going through. After all, who'd want to talk to a counsellor who makes life worse?

So if the Holy Spirit is a Counsellor, it means he listens, he understands and he helps you deal more effectively with your problems. The word 'counsellor' comes from the Greek word *paraklete*, which is made up of two words – *para* (as in parallel lines) meaning 'alongside', and *klete* meaning 'to call'. A *paraklete* is someone who is called alongside you. The Holy Spirit does all the things Jesus would do if he were standing right there next to you!

When your boy/girlfriend dumps you and you feel depressed, there is someone there to talk to and help you through.

When your parents give you a hard time and upset you, there is someone you can turn to.

When you're feeling fed up and you're not quite sure why, there is someone who will listen and understand.

The Holy Spirit helps in lots of ways. Sometimes he may speak to you and give you the solution to a problem. At other times just the fact that you're not alone, that there's someone with you, may be enough. It can be difficult to put your finger on exactly how the Holy Spirit helps. You just know, afterwards, that he did.

For example, look at how the girl telling her story at the beginning of this chapter describes her experience. Sounds to me like she met a really good counsellor! Interestingly, this girl had seen a (human!) counsellor for over two years and made very little progress. The Holy Spirit was able to make a dramatic change in just a few moments.

FORTIFIER

The word *paraklete* is also translated 'comforter'. But don't think the Holy Spirit simply comes and puts his arm round you when you're having a rough time, and whispers, 'There, there, everything will be all right.' The second half of the word 'comforter' comes from the English word 'to fortify'. This conjures up images in my mind of an army under siege. To withstand the attacks of the enemy, the troops fortify, or strengthen, their position. When you're fortified you are built up, you have extra strength, you have more courage. These are things the Holy Spirit does. He helps you face situations that previously would have caused you to chomp your fingernails off:

- Like when the school bully has decided to make you his/her next victim.
- Like when you know you need to tell one of your mates about Jesus.
- Like when you face up to the fear of starting a new school.

I was seventeen and going out with this serious babe (not very politically correct, but it accurately describes the way I felt about her). Anyway, we had been together for over six months and I was well in love. Then, at a youth camp in Norwich one Saturday night, she breaks the news that our relationship is over. Pain city.

Not only that, but by Tuesday my ex – who I still fancied, if truth be known – is going out with someone else.

Pain, mixed with anger and feelings of inadequacy.

Wednesday, I'm asked by the leader of the camp if I'll preach that evening. He wants the works – a full thirty-minute sermon. So here I am, rejected by the woman I love for one of my fellow campers, and having to preach to well over a hundred teenagers.

To you this may not sound too bad, but believe me it was rough. OK, I'd done a couple of sermons before at youth group, but not to *that* many people. I would have been petrified at the best of times, but in my present emotional state it seemed twice as bad.

Then things got worse. The leader told me that the person leading the worship that night was – you guessed it – my ex! He suggested we got together (not that sort of getting together) to go over my sermon so that she would know what songs to sing afterwards.

To cut a long story short, I resisted the temptation to preach on the subject of integrity in relationships and being considerate of other people's feelings, and I prayed like crazy. I still felt completely petrified as I got up to speak, but the Holy Spirit was with me. That night God spoke to many people, but probably more to me than anyone. I still have a video of that service to remind me that the Holy Spirit really does fortify us, even in the scariest times of life.

TEACHER

Sometimes when we read the Bible it is hard to understand exactly what's going on and how it relates to everyday life. That's quite normal. I studied the Bible intensively for three years and there are still some bits I find difficult. When I get stuck, I sometimes open a commentary or ask someone who knows a lot about the Bible to help me. Gradually, I find an *explanation* for the passage.

At other times I pray and ask God to show me how a difficult passage applies to my life. And every now and then a verse or a story will jump off the page and kick me in the guts, and I think, Wow, I've never seen that before. Usually I learn something that is directly relevant to a situation I'm in or to something that's going on in my life. It doesn't happen every day, but when it does, it's as if God himself is writing something and he's using my heart as the notepad. Or as if the Holy Spirit is saying, 'Come on, Steve, you need to learn something here.' This is *application* of the Word, by the Spirit, to our lives. This is important because God wants us to love him with all our minds, and the Holy Spirit leads us into all truth.

The difference between explanation and application is that explanation hits you in the grey stuff between your ears (or for the more academic among you, 'the seat of your intellect'), whereas application hits you in the fist-sized blood-pump in your chest ('the seat of your emotions').

The Holy Spirit reveals God's truths to us. Jesus said: 'But the Counsellor, the Holy Spirit, whom the Father will send in my name, will teach you all things and will remind you of everything I have said to you' (John 14:26).

What sorts of things does the Holy Spirit teach us?

- He teaches you that God loves you personally. He makes it real and applies the love of God to your heart as well as your mind.

God has poured out his love into our hearts by the Holy Spirit, whom he has given us. *(Romans 5:5)*

I remember when, a couple of years after I became a Christian, a visiting minister prayed for a group of us young people at church. We were all huddled together in a sort of rugby scrum when the Holy Spirit moved on us. We stood praying together for about an hour, and by the time we had finished half of us were crying. That night God filled me with his Holy Spirit. The external sign was that I cried; on the inside God poured out his love into my heart. I can honestly say that from that day to this I have never again doubted that he loved me.

- The Holy Spirit teaches you that you are a child of God. In the last chapter we looked at verses which talk about our identity as children of God. This isn't just intellectual information. The Holy Spirit reveals it to us on the inside.

Only those people who are led by God's Spirit are his children. God's Spirit doesn't make us slaves who are afraid of him. Instead, we become his children and call him our Father. God's Spirit makes us sure that we are his children. *(Romans 8:14–16)*

Now that we are his children, God has sent the Spirit of his Son into our hearts. And his Spirit tells us that God is our Father. You are no longer slaves. You are God's children, and you will be given what he has promised. *(Galatians 4:6–7)*

The Holy Spirit is a person who helps us, strengthens us and teaches us. These are just a few of the things he does in our lives. Jesus promised that the Holy Spirit would never leave us and we need never feel alone. This is a rock worth building your view of yourself on. Even if your friends leave you, the Holy Spirit won't:

John 14:16

I am not alone, I have the Holy Spirit with me.

You may want to know more about how you can experience the Holy Spirit. If you do, why not speak to your minister or youth leader? There are also lots of great youth events, such as Soul Survivor and Spring Harvest, where people would be willing to talk with you and pray that you would be continually filled with the Holy Spirit.

But the best place to find out about the Holy Spirit is in the Bible. Look back through some of the verses I have mentioned in this chapter, and look up some more for yourself. Spend some time on your own praying. Ask the Holy Spirit himself to reveal these truths to you.

9 HE LIVES IN ME – AND I IN HIM

The Lion King: Take two

Simba meets Raficki, the wise monkey, who knew his father. When Simba asks him, 'Who are you?', Raficki replies, 'The question is who are *you*?'

Raficki takes Simba to a pool and tells him that if he looks closely he will see how his father lives on in him. Simba looks at his reflection and begins to see his father's likeness.

The expression on Simba's face slowly changes. He is alive!

Raficki speaks: 'He lives in *you*.'

While Jesus was on the earth with his disciples, they had a very close relationship. The disciples had left their homes, jobs and families to be with him. They ate with him, travelled with him, laughed with him and learned from him. Their whole lives were centred round him. After three years of living together, Jesus broke the news to them that the party was over. Their time together on earth was coming to a violent end. In the following weeks he would be captured, tortured and murdered.

Imagine their shock, their shattered hopes, their disintegrating dreams. What would they do now? Who could they turn to? How could they live without him?

Jesus' actual words to his disciples are recorded in John's Gospel in a passage known as 'The Farewell Discourse'. Here he shares his future plan with them:

> 'On that day you will realise that I am in my Father, and you are in me, and I am in you.' *(John 14:20)*

This verse tells us two more important things about our identity as Christians.

- To be a Christian is to have Jesus living in you.
- To be a Christian is to live in Jesus.

When we talk of having Christ living in us, it is important to remember that the emphasis needs to be on Christ rather than on us. Having Christ in me can imply that I am bigger than Christ (leading to the dreaded ego problem). Perhaps this is why the New Testament writers concentrated more on the message that we are in Christ (for every reference to Christ being in you, there are ten for you being in Christ).

Jesus living in you

Being a Christian is not about externals. To be a Christian you don't have to wear open-toed sandals or carry a large black Bible to school everyday. Reading the Bible won't make you a Christian any more than reading *Animal Farm* will make you a pig. Going to church doesn't make you a Christian any more than going to Number 10 Downing Street makes you the Prime Minister.

When you become a Christian, something happens inside you as you invite Jesus to come into your life and forgive your sins.

[Jesus said,] 'Make up your minds to turn away from your sins. Listen! I am standing and knocking at your door. If you hear my voice and open the door, I will come in...' *(Revelation 3:20)*

A GOD-SHAPED BLANK?

The great French philosopher, Blaise Pascal, believed that at the centre of every human being was a 'God-shaped blank', a part of us that is designed to house Jesus. People without Jesus at the centre of their lives try to fill this gap with other things – perhaps sport, relationships or material possessions; perhaps drugs, alcohol or sex. These things may bring temporary pleasure but they won't bring lasting satisfaction. Without Jesus, this part of us remains unfilled, a dimension of our personality left undernourished.

It has been said that it's as if Chinese people have two stomachs, one for rice, one for other foods. Although you can feed a Chinese person on vegetables, meat and potatoes, they won't be satisfied unless they eat rice. For them, a meal is incomplete without it. It's a bit like this with us. Only Jesus can really satisfy our inner spiritual hunger.

In 1991 I read an interview with the multi-millionaire tennis star, Boris Becker. He said, 'I had won Wimbledon twice, the youngest player ever to do so ... I was rich, in effect I had all the material possessions I needed ... I know this is a cliché but I was unhappy. Everything was going badly. I saw that I had no inner calm, no peace. I was a product, a puppet on a string.'

GOOD-BYE, NORMA JEAN...

As a child Norma Jean Baker never knew who her real father was. Her mother spent much of her time in a psychiatric hospital. Norma Jean was brought up in an orphanage where she was desperately unhappy. On one occasion she ran away, only to be captured by the police and returned to the fearsome matron, Mrs Dewey. Norma Jean expected to be severely punished. But when Mrs Dewey saw her, she hugged Norma Jean, told her how pretty she was and commented on her beautiful eyes. Many years later, Norma Jean said this was the first time she felt anyone had noticed her, it was the first time she had felt loved.

Norma Jean became a model, and while she was still a teenager she was conscripted by Twentieth Century Fox to become a film star. They changed the way she dressed. They changed the way she looked. They even changed her name, the very core of her identity. They called her Marilyn Monroe.

Norma Jean's life doesn't have a happy ending. The real Norma Jean was snuffed out. She became a product of what everyone else wanted. On the outside things looked great, but inside something was missing. She died, possibly of suicide, a lonely, insecure woman. She was a classic example of the type of person who built her house on sand. When the rains came, her house crumbled and was washed away.

OUR GREATEST NEEDS ARE SPIRITUAL

Every human being has a body, a mind, the ability to have relationships, and a spirit. These are the four basic dimensions of the human personality: physical, mental, relational and spiritual.

Each dimension of our personality has basic needs. Our bodies need to be fed and exercised. Our minds need to be stimulated. We need to have loving relationships with other people. And, most importantly, we need to grow spiritually if we are to be complete.

Jesus living in us fills the gap that nothing else can fill, satisfying our spiritual needs, making us whole and complete. He promised that he would come into our lives if we ask him. When we have done this, we have a new rock on which to build our identity:

Revelation 3:20
I have Jesus living in me.

STRESSED OUT?

We live in a world that is full of pressures. Exam pressure, peer pressure, pressure from parents, pressure to succeed. Stress is an illness that affects increasing numbers of young people as well as older people. How can we survive in such a hostile environment? By realising that we have an amazing source of strength living in us. Right at the very core of our being, at the centre of our identity, is Jesus.

John, one of Jesus' disciples, knew what it was like to live in a hostile world. Before he became a follower of Jesus, he was one of the local hard-men. He and his brother were known as the 'Sons of Thunder'. John needed to be tough to survive the persecution that broke out against the church soon after Jesus' death.

One early church historian claimed that John survived being boiled in oil! What is more certain is that he spent the last years of his life in exile on the island of Patmos. Here, we believe, he wrote the book in the Bible known as 1 John, in which he gives advice on how to survive in a world of opposition and pressure. The key, he says, is to understand that Jesus lives in you. It makes an enormous difference.

> Children, you belong to God, and you have defeated
> these enemies. God's Spirit is in you and is more pow-
> erful than the one that is in the world. *(1 John 4:4)*

I was petrified when I started work in a high school. I was only twenty-two and it was my first proper job. Here I was, surrounded by over a thousand adolescents, and I had to get up in front of them in assembly and tell them who I was and why I was on their turf.

I was in my office praying like crazy, 'God, you've got to help me.' I started reading a small copy of the New Testament which I found lying around. When I came to this verse from 1 John – smack! – it hit me right between the eyes.

As I walked through the corridors during the rest of the day, I kept repeating it over and over in my mind. The result was, I stopped feeling scared out of my brains and was able to hold my head up and look people in the eye with a degree of confidence. God had got me the job in the school, and Jesus lived in me – so what was there to worry about? Suddenly I had a completely different perspective. This is another important rock:

1 John 4:4

I belong to God. God's Spirit is in me and is more powerful than the one that is in the world.

We have real strength, true strength, inner strength, because Jesus lives in us.

Think of a situation which makes you feel scared
and try repeating this verse to yourself.

Living in Christ
• • • • • • • • • • • • • •

The New Testament has a lot to say about being 'in
Christ'. You might like to look in particular at Paul's let-
ters to the Ephesians, Corinthians and Galatians. In
fact, with 40 references in Ephesians alone, many
scholars see being 'in Christ' as the number one theme
of the New Testament. To understand who we are, it is
vital that we understand what it means.

YOU BECOME 'IN CHRIST' WHEN YOU BECOME A CHRISTIAN

Jean François Gravelet, otherwise known as Blondin,
was a famous tightrope walker. He first crossed the
Niagara Falls in 1859, and went on to attempt many
more increasingly difficult crossings. He went over
blindfolded, tossing an omelette and riding on a bicycle (not all at the same time – that really would have
been something!).

His first crossing was his most famous. When he
reached the other side, the crowd were chanting his
name, 'Blondin, Blondin, Blondin!' Then Gravelet
announced that he intended to cross back over the
Falls, but this time carrying someone on his back.
People cheered. They all believed he could do it.

Then he asked for a volunteer. Everyone went
strangely quiet.

Eventually Gravelet turned to his manager, and it
was he who climbed on the tightrope walker's back to
be carried across the raging Falls.

To be a Christian is to give your whole life to Jesus.
It's not enough to stand on the sidelines and say, 'I

believe'. Becoming a Christian involves a step of faith, trusting your whole life to him. When you say, 'OK, Jesus, I'm with you now. I'll go wherever you want me to. I'm putting my life in your hands', you become 'in Christ'.

FROM ADAM TO CHRIST

Earlier, we looked at the fact that we were all of us 'in Adam'. Adam was a sinner, and we are his descendants. We inherited his sinful nature, and this means that what was true of Adam is true of us.

However, when we become Christians there is a shift. We change from being 'in Adam' to being 'in Christ'. Just as what was true of Adam was true of us, now what is true of Christ is true of us.

A WINNING COMBINATION

Imagine you're a bit of a motor-sports fan. You go along to watch some major event like the RAC rally. You position yourself on the first bend and listen to the noisy grumble of engines revving up. Eventually your hero pulls up to the line to begin the race. The flag is lowered – and they're off!

As your hero's car nears the first bend, he makes a mistake. The car spins and his co-driver takes a shuddering knock on the head against his window. Your hero sees his assistant is in no fit state to continue the race, and instantly beckons you to take his place in the passenger seat. Before you know what's happening, you're sitting next to your hero, your seat-belt securely fastened. You're in the race!

Over the next hour you experience the ultimate white-knuckle ride. Speed city! You sit there motionless, unable to give any assistance with directions, or advice on the course, or what line to take into a bend. By the time you cross the finishing line, you've bitten off all your fingernails and have fairly strong teeth indentations on three of your fingers. The good news is, your driver has won the race!

As you step out of the car, a reporter stuffs a microphone in your face and announces that you're the youngest ever co-driver to win a major championship. Your reward is a cheque for £10,000.

This is a bit like what it is to be in Christ. Because we are on his team, we get all the benefits of his achievements. We can be a winner because he's a winner. Even if our efforts are pretty useless, we're OK because it doesn't depend on us. We don't have to be some sort of super-Christian. Everything we have is based on what he has done for us and on our relationship with him.

The benefits

Say, for example, you are at some sort of youth event. You were dragged along by one of your Christian friends, and you're enjoying it – good music and a funny speaker. At the end of the service you decide you want to become a Christian. So you go and talk to someone, and they pray for you.

Things go smoothly for the first few weeks, but then you start doing stuff that you know is wrong – drinking, or drugs, or treating people badly. Afterwards, you feel terrible. You pray and ask God to forgive you. But you keep thinking there's no way you can be a Christian after what you've done. The Christian life is just too hard. You're basically not up to it. As far as you're concerned, you've messed up big-time. But the point is that you will *never* be good enough! In case you find this a tad discouraging, the good news is that being in Christ means that whether we mess up or not, we still get the benefit of everything Jesus has done.

Jesus came to earth and lived a perfect sinless life. Have you?

Thought not.

Neither have I. But I don't need to, because I am in Christ. What is true of him is true of me. Therefore it's not how holy I am that matters, it's the fact that *Christ* is very holy. If I am in Christ, then that becomes true of *me*.

So, I'm saying I'm very holy then?

Yes!!!

> Don't you know that all who share in Christ Jesus by being baptised also share in his death? When we were baptised, we died and were buried with Christ. We were baptised, so that we would live a new life, as Christ was raised to life by the glory of God the Father. (Romans 6:3–4)

When this verse speaks of baptism, it isn't just talking about being baptised in water. 'Baptism' comes from the Greek word *baptizo*. Yonks ago in Greece, this word was used when a person dipped a piece of cloth into a dye. If you had a new pair of green jeans from Top Shop and dipped them into a bowl of red dye, you would have baptised (I think this is the right Greek word – not!) your green jeans.

But why would you want to baptise your jeans? And who'd wear red jeans anyway?!

Bear with me...

Your jeans take on the colour red. In other words, they identify with the colour dye they were baptised in. We are baptised into Christ's death, so we identify with Christ's death. Our old life was crucified on the same cross; we died to ourselves, our past, our sins. On the cross Jesus defeated sin and I benefit from his victory. I don't have to win my own victory over sin. I only need to realise and believe that he has already done this for me. And then I live 'in him'.

On top of all this, Jesus was raised from the dead to new life. So we get a new life too. How? Because we are in Christ.

I like that a lot. When we are in Christ we benefit from everything he has done.

YOUR TRUE IDENTITY

There are stacks of benefits of being in Christ, but we don't have time to look at them all. Some are included in the list on page 98, along with many of the other important verses we have already turned into rocks on the way through the book. This is what God says about you, and what he says is the best foundation on which to build your identity. These Bible verses apply to *you*! As you go through them, fill your name in the blank spaces. Make a habit of reading the verses aloud each day, perhaps at the beginning of your prayer time. If you don't have prayer times, watch a bit less TV and start praying. If that doesn't work, sell your TV. (Joke! Unless you're really keen.)

As these verses sink into your consciousness, you'll discover more of what it means to be in Christ, more of what it means to have Christ in you, more of what it means to be loved and accepted as a child of God. This could be the most life-changing part of this whole book. Go back through the list now and read it aloud. Remember, it's describing who you are.

Who I am

• I made you, ..., in my image and likeness. When I saw you, I saw that you are good. *(Genesis 1:26,31)*

• I put you, ..., together inside your mother's body. You are awesomely and incredibly made. *(Psalm 139:13–14)*

• You are very dear to me, ..., and I love you. *(Isaiah 43:4)*

• You, ..., are valuable to me. *(Matthew 12:12)*

• You are my child, ..., and my friend. *(John 1:12; 15:15)*

• You are in me, ..., and I am in you. *(John 14:20)*

• I have chosen you, ... You do not belong to this world but to me. *(John 15:19)*

• I have forgiven you, ..., and made you righteous and clean. *(Romans 5:1)*

• You, ..., are free from guilt and condemnation. *(Romans 8:1)*

• You are my child, ..., and I am your dad. *(Romans 8:15–16)*

• .... I am on your side; I am for you. *(Romans 8:31)*

• You are my work of art, ..., individually created by me for a purpose. *(Ephesians 2:10)*

• You, ..., are a member of my family. *(Ephesians 2:19)*

• You, ..., are part of my chosen people, a group of royal priests, a holy nation, a special people who belong to God. *(1 Peter 2:9)*

In short

- To be a Christian is to have Jesus living in me.

- To live without Jesus is to have something missing in life. Jesus makes me a whole person.

- Having Jesus within gives me the power to live in a world full of pressure.

- To be a Christian is to live in Christ. What is true of him becomes true of me. I get to benefit from what he has done. His death becomes my death, his new life gives me new life.

My identity is built upon the fact that
I am the child of a King
Jesus lives in me
I am in Christ

10 CHANGING THE TAPES – THE BATTLEGROUND OF THE MIND

David was sitting on the hillside, playing the electric guitar he'd got for his birthday. He was working on a new song and keeping an eye on his dad's sheep at the same time.

He was interrupted by his dad, who handed him a box of pizzas. He wanted David to deliver them to his brothers who were working at the nearby army base. (This story, in its original form, is found in 1 Samuel 17.)

When David arrived, he couldn't believe his eyes. The Israelite army was lined up ready for battle on the hillside. On the other side of the valley the Philistine army stood in battle formation. The Philistines were long-time enemies of Israel. They had invaded from the Mediterranean Sea many years earlier, and now dominated the coastal areas. They were led by five kings, each of whom lived in a massive city.

The scene before him reminded David of a large crowd at a basketball match. On court, between the opposing sets of fans, stood a ten-foot giant. He was tall enough to be able to dunk with his head! He was wearing a coat of armour that weighed 125 pounds. His thick, muscular legs were protected by strips of bronze. Strapped to his side was a sword, and on his back he carried a huge javelin. He held a spear with a thick, iron tip that had pierced the hearts of many of his victims. Goliath, the heavyweight champion of the Philistines, made Arnold Schwarzenegger look like Tom Thumb.

While David looked on, Goliath shouted at the Israelites: 'Come on, then! Aren't there any men among you? Won't someone come down and fight me! If you win, we Philistines will be your slaves. If I win, you'll serve us!'

Well, you might be thinking, this is all very interesting stuff. But what's it got to do with *me*? I've never met anyone who dresses like this Goliath character. And where did he get his sad name from?

The story of David and Goliath is a sort of preview of a battle each of us is involved in. We face a different enemy, an even more fearsome one. He is not a physical being like Goliath, but a spiritual one:

> Put on all the armour that God gives, so you can defend yourself against the devil's tricks. We are not fighting against humans. We are fighting against forces and authorities and against rulers of darkness and powers in the spiritual world. So put on all the armour that God gives. Then when that evil day comes, you will be able to defend yourself.
> (Ephesians 6:11–13)

> We live in this world, but we don't act like its people or fight our battles with the weapons of this world. Instead, we use God's power that can destroy fortresses. (2 Corinthians 10:3–4)

What's this enemy like?
Forget the scarlet leotard, the horns and the three-pronged fork. The devil very seldom appears in this garb, except on TV. The enemy we face is invisible

because he is spiritual. But just because you can't see him, it doesn't mean the devil isn't real. Here's the run-down on him.

HE IS THE 'ACCUSER' (REVELATION 12:10)

Like the school bully who's always on your case, trying to make you look small. Like your worst ever teacher, the one who suffered from a severe sense of humour failure at birth and who seems to take delight in highlighting your mistakes and humiliating you. Like the lawyer representing the opposition, with you in the dock, whose aim is to grind you into the dust. Guilt is his speciality. He'll blame you for your parents' divorce. He'll blame you if you were abused. He'll try his hardest to make you feel that the things which aren't your fault, are. And sometimes the accuser can be very convincing…

HE COMES TO STEAL, KILL AND DESTROY (JOHN 10:10)

Yeah, but what does he destroy? Your confidence, your relationships with others and, most of all, your relationship with God. This is because he's mad at God and wants to hurt him badly, but he doesn't have the power to do so directly.

Imagine for a minute someone really stroppy wanted to have a go at me. Unless he (or she) was over six feet tall, this could be difficult. The best way to hurt me would be to hurt someone I love, like my wife. That would really get to me. Similarly, the only way the devil can hurt God is by trying to destroy the people God loves. By hurting you he hurts God because God loves you very much.

HE IS 'THE FATHER OF LIES' (JOHN 8:44)

The devil tells porkies, big ones. Whatever he says, don't believe it 'cos it ain't true. I know a girl who all the lads think is drop-dead gorgeous. Yet inside she's convinced she's ugly – her nose is too big, her cheek-bones aren't high enough. Interesting, isn't it, how many of the most attractive people have the lowest opinions of themselves?

How does the devil attack us?

Let's go back to the story of David and Goliath. How did Goliath attack God's people, Israel?

> Goliath went out and shouted to the army of Israel: 'Why are you lining up for battle? I'm the best sol-dier in our army, and all of you are Saul's army. Choose your best soldier to come out and fight me! If he can kill me, our people will be your slaves. But if I kill him, your people will be our slaves. Here and now I challenge Israel's whole army! Choose someone to fight me!

> Saul and his men heard what Goliath said, but they were so frightened of Goliath that they couldn't do a thing.

Goliath was a big guy. He looked mean. But at no point do we actually see a display of his strength. He doesn't maul or kill anyone. He doesn't even flex his huge biceps in public. All he does is shout.

When the Israelite army heard his words, the things he said, they got scared. So how does the devil attack us? Exactly the same way! With words.

THE TAPE BEGINS TO PLAY
You're lying in bed at night. A voice whispers in your ear: 'You're no good. You're a failure. You never do anything right. You're always messing up big-time, so

why even bother trying? You may as well give up now. Haven't you noticed you're no good at anything?

'Nobody really cares about you. How often do people want to talk to you? If anyone did bother to get to know you, they wouldn't like you anyway.

'It's your fault your dad left. He didn't love you, that's why he moved out. You're the one to blame.'

Maybe you're thinking, So what? Everyone thinks like this at some point in their lives. Is it really such a big deal?

Several times now, I've escorted young people to casualty after they have taken an overdose. Some were serious attempts, some were cries for help. In each case, as I look back over the weeks and months before the overdose, the same pattern emerges. The young person began to feel worthless and think just those kinds of thoughts. It was like a tape playing in their minds: 'You're no good. You're a loser. Nobody cares.'

Unfortunately, the longer the tape plays, the deeper the impression it makes. It stops being a normal bout of self-pity and turns into something much more damaging: 'I feel useless' becomes 'I *am* useless'. It becomes part of your identity.

Why does the devil want us to believe these things about ourselves? The Bible says, 'As a man thinks in his heart so he is.' You become what you think. If you think of yourself as a failure and a waste of space, your behaviour will reflect this and you will act like a failure, and it won't be fun for anyone to watch. The result of continually allowing the tape to play might be:

Self-mutilation
Anorexia
Bulimia

Depression
Panic attacks
Drug abuse
Giving in to peer pressure
Having casual sexual relationships
Suicide

Am I perhaps being just a tad dramatic?

Suicide is now the second biggest killer of teenagers (after car accidents) in Britain. The number of young people developing eating disorders has exploded in the last ten years. According to the Eating Disorder Association, one London hospital reports a 360% increase in the number of young people seeking medical treatment since 1988. Many television programmes have featured the 'new' phenomenon in recent years of self-mutilation, young people cutting their arms and legs with razors to relieve the pain they are feeling. All these disorders have one thing in common. They start with words playing like a tape in the mind. This is the devil's strategy to hurt you.

Is this a satanic attack or did I stub my toe in the shower?

However, not all negative thoughts are from the devil. If you stub your toe getting out of the shower, it's likely that a negative thought will pass along the neural highways of your mind. This is not necessarily a satanic onslaught!

The way to discern whether or not the thoughts in your mind are a spiritual attack is to remember that the devil is an accuser, he comes to destroy and he is a liar. Thoughts that consistently accuse, condemn or point the finger are likely to be from him. Thoughts that try to get you to hurt yourself resemble the devil's handiwork. Thoughts that aren't true can be traced back to him.

If you are having such thoughts, what can you do about it? What did David do when he was faced with Goliath?

I'm not listening to this junk

'Great,' thought David, 'it's show time. I'm going to see some action at last. This is much more fun than watching those stupid sheep.'

He hurried over to the Israelite army, and handed over the pizzas to his brothers. He wanted to find out when the fight would be on. Who would be the one lucky enough to go out and teach this guy a lesson? He hoped one of his brothers would be chosen to deliver the goods.

To his amazement he found that not one Israelite wanted to fight Goliath. They had all completely wimped out. David couldn't believe it.

'Too big to hit,' they thought to themselves.

'Too big to miss,' thought David. 'This guy's full of hot air. He's got more wind than a tin of beans. If no one else will fight him, I will. I may not look very big on the outside, but God has already taught me that it's not how big you are that counts. It's what's on the inside that really matters.'

Picture the scene.

Ding, ding! Round one.

There are two hills with a valley between them. On the left are thousands of Philistines, loving every minute. Their champion is unbeaten. The bookies have given them great odds. They're doing Mexican waves, shouting obscenities at the Israelites and chanting Goliath's name at the top of their lungs. It's party time.

On the right are thousands of Israelites, scared stiff. You can almost feel the fear as they watch David's tiny figure walk onto the battle field.

Goliath stands tall and strong, mocking his opponent. 'Is that the best you can do? I ask for your best man and you send out a pygmy? Don't you guys realise the survival of your nation is at stake?'

He looks down at David. 'This is no game, son. I'm about to rip your guts out, feed your intestines to the birds and the rest of you to the animals. Prepare to die.' (Not a very pleasant introduction.)

David stands there, wearing no armour, in one hand a small leather bag containing five smooth stones picked from the river, in the other a sling. He isn't listening to Goliath, his heart is lifted to God in prayer. Goliath may be big, but God is bigger.

'The bigger you are, the harder you're gonna fall, Goliath. You may look tough, but that doesn't scare me. The God who made the universe is on my side. Today he's going to defeat you and deliver you into my hands. Then I'm going to cut your head off.'

David strides towards Goliath, reaching into his bag as he does so. A stone drops into his sling. He begins to whirl it over his head. The Philistine hordes are roaring from the sidelines, but he is focused on Goliath. The stone shoots out of the sling and flies through the air like a laser-guided tomahawk-missile, striking Goliath between the eyes. The giant is stopped in his tracks. He sways unsteadily, his legs begin to buckle. Moments later, he falls to the ground with a mighty thud.

The Philistine crowd look on in disbelief as David walks over to Goliath's lifeless body. He takes the sword from his victim's side and, with one sweep, removes Goliath's head from his shoulders. Then, in a gesture of victory, he holds the head up in the air.

'Where are your words now, Goliath?'

THE COLISEUM OF YOUR MIND

The battle we face is not against a ten-foot giant, but against the words the enemy hits us with in our minds. Are you the champion in the coliseum of your mind? Are you a victim or a victor? Do you allow the words of the enemy to dominate your thinking, the way you see yourself? Does the tape play over and over, accusing you, trying to destroy you? Or have you, like David, engaged in battle?

You and your girl/boyfriend decide to have a night in. You hire a video, and snuggle up on the couch with a few choccies and some popcorn. You switch the video on – and sit for two hours watching utter drivel, the worst movie you've ever seen. It's a complete waste of an evening. The video looked good in the shop but it was nothing like you expected.

Anyway, the next night you and your girl/boyfriend have another evening in. You go to the video shop and look for a film. Would you pick out the one you'd borrowed the day before, take it home and spend a couple of hours watching the same old rubbish? Would you do it the next night, and the night after that? It would be stupid, wouldn't it? So why allow the same thing to happen in our minds?

The devil says, 'You're no good, you're a waste of space, nobody cares about you.' We've heard the same tape going round and round. We focus on the bad experiences from the past, the times people hurt us, the occasions when we failed or looked stupid in front of others. We allow the same tape to play over and over. And each time we hear it, we feel worse.

YOU HOLD THE REMOTE CONTROL

The first thing we need to realise is that we are responsible for what goes on in our minds. We have the remote control in our hands. We can press 'Play' or 'Stop'.

I sometimes find it helpful to picture my mind as a classroom. The thoughts are the students and I'm the teacher. What goes on in the classroom is my responsibility, I'm in charge. Of course, there are going to be times when students mess around or are rude, but I can speak authoritatively to them or send them out of the room. You can do the same with your thoughts.

When the tape begins to play in your mind, saying, 'You're worthless, you may as well be dead', press 'Stop'! Just decide, 'I'm not going to allow this to get me down any longer.'

PLAY ANOTHER TAPE

The next step is to recognise that the only way to get rid of a thought is to replace it with another. Thoughts don't disappear of their own accord: you need to start focusing on something else. But what?

I heard a psychologist recently teaching on how to achieve high self-esteem. He advised everyone to repeat the following phrase at least one hundred times each day: 'I like myself, I like myself, I like myself.'

Now if you're anything like me you'd probably feel a bit of an idiot doing this, even if you remembered not to do it out loud. So how do you replace the thoughts?

Learn to use a sword

When David flattened Goliath, he chopped off his head with a sword. In the New Testament the Bible (which is also known as God's word) is likened to a sword. It is one of the weapons at our disposal in our spiritual battle against the words of the devil in our minds.

> For the word of God is living and active. Sharper
> than any double-edged sword... *(Hebrews 4:12)*

I'm not suggesting you take the biggest Bible you can get your hands on and start waving it around whenever you feel depressed. Here's how to use the Bible in the battle against the devil.

First, take the list of verses from the end of chapter nine, and repeat these to yourself a few times each day for a week. Memorise at least ten. Once you have memorised God's word, you are better armed for the battle. You are carrying your sword.

Second, whenever the tape begins to play in your head, make the decision that *you* are in control: you are not going to allow those thoughts to beat you up. Mentally, press 'Stop', then press the 'Play' button on some of the verses you've memorised. By doing this you push the bad thoughts out and focus instead on what God says about you.

Remember, the devil is king of the accusers, he comes to destroy you, and he's a liar. God loves you, he wants to give you life, and his word is true. By focusing on God's word you change the tape in your mind! You throw out the old one and replace it with something much better.

Scud-buster

When the Gulf War broke out a few years ago, there was great concern that the Iraqis had chemical weapons at their disposal. Hospitals all over Britain prepared to receive soldiers suffering from gruesome war wounds. One of the most feared weapons was the Scud missile. During the war, hundreds of these were launched against the Allied Forces and Israel.

Similarly, the enemy we face launches Scud missiles at us, and they can cause massive damage to our thoughts, our feelings and our behaviour.

However, during the Gulf War a hero emerged. No, not Stormin' Norman Schwarzkopf, or any other military leader. The real superstar of the war was the Patriot missile. Originally an American offensive weapon, it was specially adapted to track down and intercept Scuds before they could cause any damage. The Patriot missile saved thousands of lives.

God has provided us with defensive weaponry to intercept the enemy's attacks. I like to think of the Bible as a sort of Patriot missile, a Scud-buster. You don't have to allow the devil's missiles to land unopposed in the battleground of your mind, causing untold damage. Fight back! Use your Scud-buster every day.

Martin had a problem and went to his youth leader for help. He was a committed Christian, but he kept having to battle against lustful thoughts. The youth leader spent half an hour talking to him, and discovered it was more of a problem at certain times of the day, like when Martin took a shower or went to bed at night. The youth leader shared the 'changing the tape' concept with Martin and gave him five Bible verses to memorise that week. Martin did this for a month, and each week talked with his leader to keep track of how he was getting on.

Although Martin struggled at first, he found it helped. Whenever he took a shower, instead of mentally undressing girls or film stars, he would repeat aloud the verses he'd memorised. No one could hear him because of the sound of the shower. After a few weeks he became the champion in the coliseum of his own mind. He managed to break a habit that he'd struggled with for years.

Question

Have you memorised any of the verses we've looked at in the book so far? Do it!

II WHO AM I?
THE ANSWER

'OK, God, you've got a job for me to do. Great! This shepherding lark doesn't half do your head in after a bit. So what's it involve?'

Moses sits quietly, listening while God outlines his new job description. (For this bit of the Moses saga, see Exodus 3.) When he's finished, Moses isn't too happy.

'Maybe to you this is no big deal, you being so big and powerful and all that, but this is hardly just another day at the office, is it? It's not every day someone instructs an eighty-year-old shepherd to go back to the country where he's wanted for murder and tell the most powerful king on the face of the earth to sort his life out!

'Correct me if I'm wrong, but you want *me* to tell old Pharaoh that he's got to free the three million Israelites he's been holding as slaves for the past few hundred years. I'm not allowed to buy their freedom, oh no, you're not going to give me an army or the latest high-tech weapons system. The only weapon I get to carry is a staff. With all due respect, that's hardly going to send shivers down his spine!

'And when Pharaoh gives the OK, I'm supposed to lead these three million people across the desert, without any packed lunches or a drive-thru in sight, until we come to a land which just happens to be packed full of fierce gangs who aren't going to take too kindly to us turning up on their turf. This is what you're saying to me, isn't it, God?

'Call me Mister Picky, but don't you think this is a little bit much to expect? Aren't there any other jobs going, you know, like bishop, or head of a Bible college? Caretaker perhaps?'

Moses stops and has a think. He realises it's no joke. He has become a key player in the plans and purposes of the Eternal God. He falls to his knees. The tone of his voice changes: 'I can't do this, Lord, I'm sorry. It's too much for me. I can't face Pharaoh. I can't lead three million people. Why did you have to choose *me*? I'm no good. Who am I, God? Who am I?'

If this question was addressed to a modern-day Mr Motivator, he would probably say, 'You can do it. It's a question of focus. Believe in yourself. This is *not* a crisis. It's an opportunity. Set yourself goals. Visualise yourself succeeding. Tell yourself, "I like myself, I like myself…" You can do it. You are awesome. Think it, believe it, then you'll be it!'

What God didn't say

God didn't respond like this to Moses' question. Remember, it's the question I asked you to consider back in chapter one.

- Who do you think you are?
- Are you worth anything?
- Do you have any value?
- Are you important?

When God responds, he doesn't point to any outstanding abilities or physical characteristics that Moses possesses. He doesn't say 'Chill out, Mo! Pharaoh will take one look at your 48-inch chest and sign on the dotted line.'

I'm rather glad about that, actually. I'm the sort of person who has no illusions about his physique. Once, when I was visiting my mum in hospital, a very dear old lady said I looked like a Greek god – but she had just recovered from a major operation and was high on morphine at the time. I'm not exactly an oil-painting features-wise either, and when I stand up to do a school assembly, there are no screams from the crowd, no students running forward to touch me. I am married to a very attractive wife, but when most people see us I can tell they're thinking, 'He's done well to get her.' (When I was in the States someone called me an 'over-achiever'.)

Isn't it great that we don't have to build our view of ourselves on our physical appearance? God certainly doesn't. So next time you're getting ready to go out and you don't quite manage to look like the latest sex-goddess, don't worry!

If you do happen to be blessed with perfect looks and a great body, even that's not sufficient. If physical appearance is enough to build your view of yourself on, then how come many of the prettiest girls feel so naff about themselves? What about the Naomi Campbells and Norma Jean Bakers of this world?

What God did say

Cut back to Moses. How did God answer his question, 'Who am I?'

'Don't worry about who *you* are, Moses. *I'm* with you,' God says. 'Who you are is not that important. The fact that I am going to be with you *is*.'

Moses says, 'Yeah, that's fine for me and fine for you, because you know me and I know you. The people are about to be introduced to me, but they don't know who *you* are. What should I tell them? "This is God. He's just mastered spontaneous combustion and a new line in ultra-slow burning logs?" (You know, all the burning bush stuff.) What should I say about you?'

God's reply? 'I AM WHO I AM. This is what you are to say to the Israelites: "I AM has sent me to you." Tell them "The Lord, the God of your fathers – the God of Abraham, the God of Isaac and the God of Jacob – has sent me to you."'

Notice that the question has changed. The basis for Moses' mission isn't who he is but who God is. And the name God chooses to reveal to Moses is 'I AM WHO I AM'. A strange name, but it reflects who God is – the only being who is self-sufficient, who was not created like everything else in the universe. He can exist completely whole on his own. Everything else depends on him.

Who I am really depends on 'I am WHO I am'

Our identity isn't built on who we are and what we can do, but on who God is and what God has done. This is the number one issue, the foundation for all our self-esteem. Self-esteem isn't really anything to do with self or how wonderful we are. This is why, as Christians, we need to keep humble.

If your self-esteem is built on who God is, what he has done and who he says you are, then there's only one more factor that's important – your relationship with God.

I'm on a mission from God

Moses turned to God and said, 'OK, I think we're getting somewhere here. It doesn't depend on the size of my biceps but on your strength and who you are. That's reassuring. I'll tell them your name and about all the stuff you've done in the past.

'But is that going to be enough? What if they turn round and say, "So what, Moses? We know that God is powerful, but we don't know that he's picked *you* for this task. Give us some proof that you know God personally." Lord, I need some evidence to take with me, something to show them that me and you are in this together, sort of tight.'

In Exodus 4, God gives Moses two signs to prove to Pharaoh and the Israelites that he has a relationship with God – the ability to turn his staff into a snake, and the ability to contract and heal leprosy simply by reaching for the wallet in his inside pocket. God doesn't guarantee these things will convince Pharaoh and the Israelites, but they will at least show them that Moses has a relationship with God.

The only way we can have a healthy self-esteem is by making sure we have a close, intimate relationship with God, and knowing him as our Father and friend.

It has nothing to do with your performance

'OK, God, I'm almost there. It's not who I am that's important, it's who you are. I can show them that I know you – they're pretty neat tricks you've given me, I've got to hand it to you.

'There's just one more thing. I'm scared stiff of talking in front of people. I just can't do the preachy bits, Lord, I'm sorry.'

God, who is getting a bit fed up with Moses' excuses, replies, 'Who makes people able to speak or unable to speak? Who gives them sight or makes them blind? Don't you know that I am the one who does these things? Now go! When you speak, I will be with you and give you the words to say.

'What about your brother Aaron? He will speak to

the people for you, and you will be like me, telling Aaron what to say. I will be with both of you, and I will will tell each of you what to do.'

Our performance doesn't matter: it's our obedience God is looking for. All the necessary attributes and abilities for action can be found in God, not in us. What's important is that we believe this and concentrate on trusting him.

God doesn't ask Moses for a detailed CV of his academic qualifications or his employment history. He's not bothered about whether Moses can do a dunk (this appears to be the number one measurement of masculinity among young males in America). God is looking for Moses to make God the only foundation he is prepared to build on.

Even if you smash your head off a diving board, he will love you

Greg Louganis is one of the greatest divers in modern times. He sprang to fame when, as he was competing in the Olympic Games, he smashed his head on the diving board during a particularly difficult dive. He still went on to win the gold medal. After the event, he was asked how he coped with the stress of competition. He replied, 'Even if I blow this dive, my mother will still love me.'

As God's children, there is great news for all of us. Even though we blow it from time to time, our Father in heaven still loves us and we can still feel special in his sight. Nothing depends on our performance or our appearance. Everything depends on God.

The apostle Paul, writer of one quarter of the New Testament, hero missionary and general spiritual superstar, shows us what he built his identity upon. Near the end of a very successful Christian life he writes, 'God was kind! He made me what I am' (1 Corinthians 15:10).

Never Forget

If you forget everything else you've read in this book, make sure you remember this. You're special. You're valuable. You're of incredible worth. I don't know what your parents have said to you, how your friends treat you or how attractive you are. I do know you're special because God says you are, and he never lies. Who are you going to believe? Your feelings? Your experience of life? Or God? It's your choice.

A teenager in heaven

An ordinary teenager was taken to heaven. She wasn't dead, but she might as well have been. She spent most of her time putting herself down, talking about how useless she was, telling herself she'd never amount to anything and wishing she'd never been born.

She attended church and was supposed to be a Christian, but it didn't seem to make much difference. Finally, God had had enough and summoned an angel to bring her to heaven for a chat.

The angel explained on the way up what was going to happen, and she looked forward to meeting God. She had lots she wanted to ask him. Why hadn't he made her better looking? Why didn't she have any friends? What sort of world had he created for people to live in? Most of all, she wanted to ask him why she felt so worthless all the time.

For some reason, as she stood in front of God on his throne, she was completely speechless. She couldn't think straight. She had never felt like this before. The closer she got to God, the better she felt about herself. It was weird. Her questions didn't seem to matter now.

'You wanted to know why you feel so worthless all the time, if I'm such a loving God,' he said. (God knows everything about us, even our thoughts.)

She nodded.

'I gave you a precious gift, the gift of life.' There was a pause.

'I gave you my Son. He left my side and I watched him die a cruel death for you.' (As God said this, the teenager saw for the first time how much it had really cost him to send his Son.)

'I made it possible for you to have a relationship with me. I loved you as if you were my only child, despite all your moaning. I sent my Holy Spirit to help you and strengthen you. He showed you that you had a new start, that all the mistakes from the past were gone.

'Take a look around.'

She glanced at the dazzling colours. They took her breath away. Never in her wildest dreams had she imagined heaven would be like this.

'All this I made for you, to live here for ever in a place where there will be no more rejection, no more bullying, no more depression.'

God shook his head. He looked deep into her eyes before speaking once more.

'I did all this to show you how much I value you, how much I care, that you're special to me…

'What more could I have done?'

It was a question to which she had no answer.

APPENDIX

Did you know...?

- Your body contains 55,000 miles of blood vessels. Stretched out end to end, they would circle the earth more than twice. The body has been designed so that no tissue is more than 1/500th of an inch away from a blood vessel.

- Your heart is approximately the size of your fist and weighs about the same as a can of beans. Yet, in your lifetime it will probably pump more than 500,000,000 litres of blood, equal to 18,000 petrol tankers which, if they were parked end to end, would stretch from London to Cardiff. During the seven hours that you sleep, your heart will pump enough blood to fill 56 baths.

- The juices in your stomach are strong enough to dissolve zinc, and would have no trouble burning a hole through your skin. There are 35 million glands in your stomach lining, which produce 5 pints of gastric juice every day. The acid doesn't have a chance to burn away the stomach lining, as it is renewed at the rate of half a million cells every minute, replacing itself fully every three days.

- Your skin is flaking away at such a rate that we replace our whole skin every 50 days.

- When you sneeze, air is expelled through your nose at up to 100 miles an hour. You automatically close your eyes as a natural reflex which prevents them popping out of your head. The sneeze removes irritating particles in the nose and windpipe.

- A piece of your bone the size of a matchbox can support 9 tonnes in weight. Your bone structure is four times stronger than concrete in resisting compression, even though bones are basically hollow. If they were not, we would be so heavy we wouldn't be able to move.

Is it any wonder that the psalmist said, 'I am awesomely and wonderfully made'?

Your brain

At your disposal, in the area between your two ears, is the most incredible computer on this planet.

If you look under a microscope, you will discover that your brain is made up of billions of tiny cells called *neurones*. Each one resembles a spindly octopus with many arms weaving outwards from the centre of the cell. Each single neurone is like a tiny computer cable, capable of processing one million pieces of information. The individual neurones connect with each other via their long spindly arms known as *dendrites*. At the ends of the dendrites there are tiny suckers known as the *synapse*. When the dendrites from one cell connect with those from another, like millions of octopuses joining arms, the synapse (suckers) link together, allowing a tiny electrical current to be transferred from one to another. Each single neurone can connect with 10,000 other cells!

One professor attempted to calculate the total

number of connections within the brain. He worked out that it equalled a 1 followed by 10.5 kilometres of typed zeros:

10000000000000000000000000000000000000000000
00000000000000000000000000000000000000000000
00000000000000000000000000000000000000000000
00000000000000000000.... (+ another 9.99999km)

In less time than it takes you to blink (20 milliseconds), your brain can simultaneously process between ten thousand and one million pieces of information. Compare this to a computer, which can only process one piece of information at a time. It is calculated that your brain can process thirty billion pieces of information per second.

While you are sitting reading this book, your brain is busily processing thousands of pieces of information.

Your eyes
Your eyes are a miracle of engineering. At the back of them is a small panel the size of your thumbnail, which contains 150 million light receivers. Each one can process millions of tiny light energy particles which enter every second. To regulate the appropriate flow of light into these sensors, the brain adjusts the size of the pupil so that just the right amount of light enters.

Your ears
The brain is also receiving information from your hearing system via the auditory nerve. Hearing is something we do automatically, without thinking. The outer ear acts like a funnel catching sound. The sound passes through the vibrating eardrum which is a tiny piece of skin stretched tightly. The sound is transmitted into the middle ear, where the three smallest bones in the body

are located – the hammer, anvil and stirrup. They are so perfectly tuned that they remain exactly the same size the whole of our lives and never grow or age like the other bones in our body. If you were to strike middle C on a tuning fork, these bones would vibrate 256 times per second.

From there the sound is carried into the inner ear which, although no bigger than a hazelnut, contains as many circuits as the telephone system in an average British city. The cochlea is a coiled tube filled with liquid. Inside are 24,000 strings which vibrate like piano strings. The sound is picked up by the auditory nerve linked to the brain and there we hear the sound. This whole process happens in fraction of a second.

While you're reading this book, you probably can't hear much going on around you. If you stop and listen, how many different sounds can you actually make out? Your brain receives all these but screens them through a special filter system so you can continue to concentrate on reading. But if something out of the ordinary happens, like someone calling your name, your brain will pass this information on to you so you can respond.

Wot a lot!

At the same time, your brain is doing a complex set of calculations every split second. For you to survive, your brain regulates the speed of your heartbeat and your breathing. It ensures that the right amount of fuel and energy is released at appropriate times. If you get up and start exercising, your brain will release more energy and increase your heart rate.

All this, and lots more, is going on right now while you quietly sit reading this book! Awesome or what!

How much is my body worth?

If our body is such an amazing creation, what possible

value would we place on it? What is it really worth in money terms? What would a computer doing all the things our brain can do, be worth?

Imagine, you are walking to school, when an enormous and very expensive looking car pulls up alongside you. Out steps a wealthy looking gentleman, who tells you that you have been chosen to take part in a special scientific experiment.

This multi-million pound experiment is the first of its kind, and is destined to go down in history as the beginning of a scientific revolution. Scientists are going to produce a human being from body parts donated by 100 lucky participants.

The gentleman gives you a list of body parts you can choose to donate. Once you have decided on a part, you can 'name your price', any sum you think is reasonable compensation for the inconvenience of losing a body part. He emphasises that money is no object, the important thing is that you come up with how much you think your body is worth.

You decide to donate your eyes. After all, plenty of blind people live happy lives.

What would you find difficult to do if you were blind? How much money would you want to be paid before you would choose to live like that for the rest of your life? Recently, I saw an article on the news about someone who had been awarded half a million pounds in damages after they had lost their eyesight in a workplace accident. Would you like to swap places with that person? If not, then your eyes alone are worth at least half a million!

Write down a figure based on how much you think your eyes are worth.

Here's a list of other body parts. Write a rough amount next to each one, then add up the total at the bottom.

Legs	£..................................
Facial muscles	£..................................
Ears	£..................................
Fingers	£..................................
Knee caps	£..................................
Teeth	£..................................
Hair	£..................................
Tongue	£..................................
Nose	£..................................
Vocal chords	£..................................
Total	£..................................

Hang on to your kidneys

If you think this exercise seems unreal, bear in mind that organ-selling does go on today in some parts of the world. When I was in America recently, a friend told me about an incident in New Orleans, dubbed America's 'Sin City'. A man went back to a hotel room with a woman, who then drugged him. When he awoke in the morning, he couldn't move his legs. He managed to call an ambulance from his bed. When he was examined in hospital, the doctors broke the bad news to him that one of his kidneys had been removed! The kidney had probably been sold privately to fetch tens of thousands of dollars.

I contacted an insurance company on the telephone to see how much compensation I would receive if I was involved in an accident. If I lost one limb (an arm or a leg), I would receive £37,500. If I lost both limbs, I would receive £75,000. If I lost both arms and both legs, I would receive £150,000. If I lost my sight and my hearing, this would entitle me to a further £150,000. Even something less serious like losing the use of my shoulder or a finger would entitle me to £12,000. So far this adds up to at least £300,000.

Consider how much the whole of your body is worth, including all the vital organs such as your heart, brain, liver and lungs. You are a very valuable commodity indeed.

A professor at the University of Washington attempted to work out the value of an average-sized man. He took a chemical-supply catalogue and found that the 40 grams of myoglobin in your blood would be worth £70,000. The clotting agent prothrobin would be worth £20,000. Each pint of blood donated to a Bloodmobile contains albumin worth over £600.

Professor Harold Morowitz of Yale University (the American equivalent of Oxford or Cambridge) calculated that your body is worth £158 per gram of dry weight. This means that an average-sized person is worth £4 million in chemicals alone!

On top of this, it is generally recognised that the sum of the whole is greater than the value of the parts. For example, if you dismantled a car and sold each piece one by one, the chances are you wouldn't get as much as if you sold the whole car fully operational, with all parts working together.

Are you beginning to see how much your body is worth?